Master Classes in Education Series

Testing: Friend or Foe?
The Theory and Practice of Assessment and Testing

Paul J. Black

 The Falmer Press

(A member of the Taylor & Francis Group)
London • Washington, D.C.

UK   Falmer Press, 1 Gunpowder Square, London EC4A 3DE
USA   Falmer Press, Taylor & Francis Inc., 1900 Frost Road, Suite 101, Bristol,
          PA 19007

First published in 1998

**A catalogue record for this book is available from the British
Library**

**Library of Congress Cataloging-in-Publication Data are
available on request**

ISBN 0 7507 0729 1 cased
ISBN 0 7507 0614 7 paper

Jacket design by Caroline Archer

Typeset in 11/13 Garamond and printed by
Graphicraft Typesetters Ltd., Hong Kong.

Contents

Series Editors' Preface

It has become a feature of our times that an initial qualification is no longer seen to be adequate for life-long work within a profession and programmes of professional development are needed. Nowhere is the need more clear than with respect to education, where changes in the national schooling and assessment system, combined with changes in the social and economic context, have transformed our professional lives.

The series, *Master Classes in Education*, is intended to address the needs of professional development, essentially at the level of taught masters degrees. Although aimed primarily at teachers and lecturers, it is envisaged that the books will appeal to a wider readership, including those involved in professional educational management, health promotion and youth work. For some, the texts will serve to up-date their knowledge. For others, they may facilitate career reorientation by introducing, in an accessible form, new areas of expertise or knowledge.

The books are overtly pedagogical, providing a clear track through the topic, thus making it possible to gain a sound grasp of the whole field. Each book familiarizes the reader with the vocabulary and the terms of discussion, and provides a concise overview of recent research and current debates in the area. While it is obviously not possible to deal with every aspect in depth, a professional who has read the book should be able to feel confident that they have covered the major areas of content, and discussed the different issues at stake. The books are also intended to convey a sense of the future direction of the subject and its points of growth or change.

In each subject area, the reader is introduced to different perspectives and to a variety of readings of the subject under consideration. Some of the readings may conflict, others may be compatible but distinct. Different perspectives may well give rise to different lexicons and different bibliographies, and the reader is always alerted to these differences. The variety of frameworks within which each topic can be construed is then a further source of reflective analysis.

The authors in this series have been carefully selected. Each person is an experienced professional, who has worked in that area of education as a practitioner and also addressed the subject as a researcher and theoretician. Drawing upon both pragmatic and the theoretical aspects of their experience, they are able to take a reflective view while preserving a sense of what occurs, and what is possible, at the level of practice.

Testing: Friend or Foe?

No one is better qualified to write about assessment than Professor Paul Black. In his capacity as Joint Coordinator of the Nuffield A-Level Physics Project he was in the forefront of developing a new approach to the teaching and learning of the subject. Such curriculum innovation demanded attention to what was taught, how it was taught, and how it was assessed. These three components had to be coherent and also consistent with the educational aims underlying the new curriculum. Later on, his work with the Assessment of Performance Unit involved him in developing test instruments which could be employed nationally to provide a snapshot of overall achievement. As Chairman of the Task Group on Assessment and Testing (TGAT) he was involved in advising government ministers on national policy in this area. In writing about these initiatives in this book he is able to write from direct personal experience.

The book provides an authoritative, up-to-date and accessible account of testing processes. For readers less at ease with statistical tools an introductory section is provided as an appendix. The coverage is comprehensive such that the text can serve as a standard work on contemporary thinking about assessment procedures.

It is an important factor that in writing this book Paul Black was not solely concerned in generating an accurate technical account but also in bringing out the underlying humanistic significance of testing. Education is a humanistic enterprise. Assessment procedures can inhibit this essential quality. Testing may dominate the work so that teachers will solely be concerned with working with test outcomes in mind. Further distortion can arise in the interpretation of test data so that special interest groups can selectively use the material as evidence to advance their cause. However, testing can have positive outcomes. By looking at where and why students get things wrong we can diagnose the likely causes of error and then use thus information to guide our pedagogy. In this sense, assessment remains one of the most useful tools to help teachers in their work. It is, indeed, their friend.

John Head
Ruth Merttens
Series Editors

Acknowledgments

Colleagues too numerous to mention have contributed to my education in this subject over the years, so that it would be invidious to select a few names. For help with the text of this book, I owe particular thanks to Dr Tony Mansell whose careful reading and criticism did much to improve Chapter 2, and to Dr John Head, who has exercised his oversight as a series editor with a blend of criticism, support and patience which helped me to want to do better. However, for the outcomes of my efforts in these pages I bear sole responsibility.

Chapter 1

Introduction

The Aim of this Book

As I write this introduction, there are about fifty books on assessment on and around my desk, and this is only a fraction of the number on the library shelves. So a book like this one can only be an introduction to the academic study of assessment. It is designed to be a comprehensive introduction. My strategy is to attempt to convey a grasp of the most important concepts, and to then convey some introductory acquaintance with the many conceptual, technical and practical issues that follow. Where the treatment has to be so short that it is superficial, I hope that the bibliography and references will guide readers who look for more thorough treatments.

My own experiences, as a university teacher and examiner; as an A-level examiner with two GCE boards; as a member of the board and of the research committee for one of those boards; as one of the directors of the science monitoring of the Assessment of Performance Unit (APU); and as chair of the 1987–88 Task Group on Assessment and Testing (TGAT), have all fashioned my particular perspective on this subject. However, whilst I draw on these resources, particularly from the APU work, to illustrate the ideas, analyses of these particular experiences lie outside the scope of this book. Thus, for example, readers will have to look elsewhere for my attempts to reflect on the experiences of the APU work (Black, 1990) or of the TGAT venture (Black, 1993, 1994, 1997). In the same spirit, this book does not attempt to focus closely on any analysis of the developments in national assessment in the UK following from the 1988 Education Reform Act, except to refer to some of the developments as illustrations of basic issues and, of course, to give reference to fuller treatments by others. The discussion does draw upon the experience of other countries, partly because this broadening of perspective shows up some of the issues more clearly, and partly because it is important to question and explore what one has come to take for granted about one's own experience.

Structure and Sequence

In any study of curriculum and pedagogy in education, the issues involved in assessment and testing cannot be understood as marginal extras. As the

Friend or Foe?

Figure 1:   *An outline of the book — three main strands*

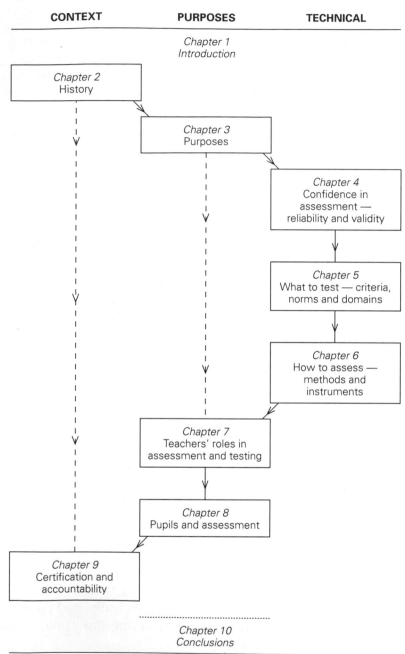

arguments in this book should make clear, assessment and testing should be the heart of any such study. As the TGAT report (DES, 1988 paragraph 3) declared:

> Promoting children's learning is a principal aim of schools. Assessment lies at the heart of this process. It can provide a framework in which educational objectives may be set, and pupils' progress charted and expressed. It can yield a basis for planning the next educational steps in response to children's needs.

However, there is far more involved. Clear and compelling principles are not enough to guide the establishment of assessment practices. These practices can only be understood in relation to the historical, cultural and political contexts within which they are worked out, and they also entail complex issues both of technique and of principle.

The way in which these issues are worked through in this book is illustrated by *Figure 1*. There are three main themes or strands, represented by the three vertical columns. The left hand strand is the general social context. Here, some historical and cultural foundations are explored in Chapter 2 by a presentation of two brief and contrasting histories — of assessment and testing in England and in the USA respectively. The central strand is concerned with purposes. Chapter 3 sets the scene for the core exploration of the issues, both of principle and of technique, with a discussion of the three main purposes of assessment — the formative, the summative and the accountability purposes respectively.

The right hand strand is concerned with technical issues, which are covered by three chapters in succession. Chapter 4 discusses the concepts of reliability and validity, with particular reference to links between validity and assumptions about effective learning. In the light of these key criteria, Chapter 5 explores what assessment results are actually designed to tell us, an issue which underlies the technical issues of norm referencing, and of criterion and domain referencing. Chapter 6 then looks more closely at the practicalities with a survey of the different methods which can be used for assessment — ranging from the various types of questions used in written test papers to the recording of classroom performance.

Chapter 7 comes back to the links between purposes and general policy with a discussion of teachers' roles in assessment, giving particular emphasis to formative assessment but also leading in to debates about teachers' roles in summative assessment. Chapter 8 takes this same exploration further by looking closely at pupils' roles in assessment, in particular at the development of self-assessment by pupils.

The summative aspects, which serve the certification and accountability purposes, are then discussed more fully in Chapter 9. Thus, this chapter adds to the discussions of purposes, but the ways in which these purposes are achieved can only be appraised by looking at national systems within which policies for assessment, curriculum and accountability are interrelated. For this reason, this chapter gives examples from several different countries. In doing this, and probing more deeply into the issues surrounding accountability and the rhetoric of standards, it brings the discussion back to the broader perspectives introduced in Chapter 2. Chapter 10 then gives a closing summary, emphasizing particularly the need for a systemic approach to any reform of assessment.

Organization of the Chapters

Each chapter has both an introduction, to explain the structure and sequence of its sections and sub-sections, and a summary which draws together the main points that have been explored.

The links which will help you to explore the literature are given in two forms. At the end of each chapter there is both a bibliography and a set of references. The bibliography lists books or review articles which would be useful sources to follow up the issues of the chapter in more detail, and also to see them presented from different perspectives. Where appropriate, some indication is given of the chapters in each book which are particularly relevant.

Whilst the bibliography gives a general guide to treatments by other authors, the set of references listed are very specific guides for following up particular points made in the present text. These are therefore linked to explicit references in the text. Where the reference is to a particular chapter or set of pages this will be indicated either in the text or in the reference list.

The bibliography and reference lists for each chapter are self-contained, in that they do not depend or draw upon the corresponding lists from other chapters. So, for example, some books will appear in the bibliographies for several chapters — each chapter referring to different parts of the same book, whilst others may only appear for the one chapter for which their particular treatment gives a useful expansion.

Words, Words, Words

Most difficulties about terminology have been dealt with as the need to introduce words with unusual or difficult meanings arises. However, two particular problems arise throughout and need particular introduction.

The first is presented by the terms 'assessment' and 'testing'. These overlap, can often be taken to mean the same thing, and carry different overtones, 'testing' being hard, rigorous, inflexible and narrow-minded, 'assessment' being soft, sensitive, and broad- or woolly-minded. Other authors have met the same difficulty:

Note that I use the term test when referring to traditional, standardised developmental and pre-academic measures and the term assessment when referring to more developmentally appropriate procedures for observing and evaluating young children. This is a semantic trick that plays on the different connotations of the two terms. Technically, they mean the same thing. (Shepard, 1994)

It is to be hoped that the overtones can be set aside, but the position adopted here is that whilst the two terms overlap, they do not mean the same thing. The terms are to be used according to the following definitions provided in the glossary of the TGAT report:

Assessment: A general term embracing all methods customarily used to appraise performance of an individual pupil or group. It may refer to a broad appraisal including many sources of evidence and many aspects of a pupil's knowledge, understanding, skills and attitudes; or to a particular occasion or instrument. An assessment instrument may be any method or procedure, formal or informal, for producing information about pupils: for example, a written test paper, an interview schedule, a measurement task using equipment, a class quiz.

Test: Strictly, any assessment conducted within formal and specified procedures, designed to ensure comparability of results between different test administrators and between different test occasions. For some it implies a set of written questions, externally prescribed, with written responses marked according to rigid rules; for others, any of a broad range of assessment instruments with standardised rules of administration and marking which ensure comparability of results. This report uses the term in this latter, broader sense. (see the Glossary in DES, 1988)

The second problem concerns the words used to refer to those involved in the assessment process. I shall use teachers throughout: the main emphasis here is on assessment in schools. Much of what is being said will be applicable to higher education and to employment, although the particular needs and problems in those spheres are not directly addressed.

I shall also use the terms 'pupils' and 'students' to refer to those who enjoy or suffer assessment or testing practices. To use 'students' for very young children in primary or pre-primary education could be confusing, whereas to use 'pupils' for A-level candidates seems inappropriate. However, in principle these terms will be interchangeable.

Statistics

It is not difficult to find works on assessment which are replete with algebraic equations and heavy with the technical language and concepts of statistics. Whilst there are sound reasons for the deployment of this machinery in assessment studies, very little of it is required for this book's purpose. A qualitative understanding of the following terms will be assumed:

Mean	Normal distribution	Spread
Standard deviation	Correlation	Regression

Explanation of these terms for the beginner is given in the Appendix, together with some useful references to other texts.

Attitudes and Outlooks

All who read this book will have experienced assessment and testing — at least as their recipients (victims?) and probably as their agents. Few will regard either of these sets of experiences as happy memories. Thus, it is to be expected that a book about the subject can hope for no more than to arouse morbid fascination, rather than to give pleasure. Being an optimist, this author hopes for more. The subject is inescapably central to any educational enterprise. Those who can grasp the concepts that underpin it, and who can explore the alternatives for practice that are possible, will be better equipped for all educational work, and might even be able to turn at least some experiences of assessment into enjoyable aspects of learning.

References

BLACK, P.J. (1990) 'APU Science — the past and the future', *School Science Review*, **72**, 258, pp. 13–28.

BLACK, P.J. (1993) 'The shifting scenery of the National Curriculum', in O'HEAR and WHITE, J. (eds) *Assessing the National Curriculum*, London: Paul Chapman, pp. 57–69.

BLACK, P.J. (1994) 'Performance assessment and accountability: The experience in England and Wales', *Educational Evaluation and Policy Analysis*, **16**, pp. 191–203.

BLACK, P.J. (1997) 'Whatever happened to TGAT?', in Cullingford, C. (ed.) *Assessment versus Evaluation*, London: Cassell, pp. 24–50.

DEPARTMENT OF EDUCATION AND SCIENCE (1988) *Task Group on Assessment and Testing — National Curriculum: A Report*, London: Department of Education and Science.

SHEPARD, L. (1994) 'The challenges of assessing young children appropriately', *Phi Delta Kappan*, November, pp. 206–10.

Chapter 2

History

Why Bother?

It may seem strange to choose a historical review for the first substantive chapter of this book. A first justification is that in general the terms, methods and procedures used in assessment and testing in any country can only be understood in the light of that country's historical development, in relation both to its education system and to broader social factors. It follows that such terms, methods and procedures have to be understood in terms of their particular national contexts and should not be seen as universals framed in an internationally unambiguous framework of understanding.

There is, however, a second reason which follows from the first. Any reader is bound to bring to these chapters a set of assumptions, about meanings of terms and about the norm for procedures and systems, which may not be shared with other readers, or even with myself as author. The differences here can run deep and can lead to breakdowns in communication which are the more difficult to repair because a superficial agreement might preclude any attention to their existence.

It is also important to see any account of assessment as a snapshot, one frame of a record which moves on, perhaps slowly, perhaps quickly, according to the impact of a variety of pressures. The account in this book will be set in my perspective so that, whilst I strive for a higher plane of objectivity to make the account universal and enduring, any success will only be partial.

The approach used here will be to give first a brief account of the oldest recorded examination system, that of China, and to then focus on two historical sketches, one of the development of assessment in England in the nineteenth and twentieth centuries, the other in a corresponding history for the USA. Whilst the selection will serve to bring out some of the main lessons, the result must be seen as a limited venture, ignoring many other times and many other cultures.

Examinations in China

The first historical records of testing as a means of selection date from over 2000 years ago. Successive dynasties in China developed formal written tests as the mode of entry into the civil service, a profession carrying the highest prestige and power in the country. Almost all of the population could enter, and the system ensured that test attainment, rather than parentage or patronage, was the avenue to success. Tens of thousands of candidates were examined annually and there was a continual struggle to prevent various forms of cheating. However, the examinations came to test largely memory of received wisdom, mainly about the Confucian classics. One historical study concluded that:

> Instead of wise and morally outstanding representatives of government authority the system supplied incompetent officials, ignorant of the ways of the world; instead of an intellectual aristocracy (it supplied) a class of ignorant and narrow minded literati. (Franke, quoted p. 191 in Hanson, 1993)

The system was abolished in 1905 having been an important social instrument for over 1000 years. Its demise came as part of a wholesale reform of the educational system as part of an attempt to modernize many aspects of Chinese society.

Assessment and Testing in England

The Professions

The history to be sketched here starts with the profound changes which saw the widespread introduction of written tests in England in the nineteenth century. Introducing his edited collection of studies of the early history of assessment, Roy MacLeod (1982) wrote:

> As John Roach has observed, 'Public examinations were one of the great discoveries of nineteenth century Englishmen'. This discovery rested in large on the belief that competitive, open, and increasingly written examinations would eventually remove the undesirable consequences of unregulated favouritism, and would, if universally extended, have a salutary influence on society generally. (p. 1)

Prior to this 'discovery' entrance to universities and access to many of the professions depended on a variety of informal routes. Oral examinations, formal and informal, played their part, but patronage, 'friends at court', and traditional family and class elites provided most of the avenues. The need for something different arose for some from the need for social justice, for others from the pressures of a developing society which needed far more trained professionals and a more literate work-force than the old avenues could supply, and for others again, notably in the professions and the universities, from anxiety to raise the standards of their institutions. Thus, a statement by the British Association for the Advancement of Science in 1903 summed up the effect of the changes as follows:

> . . . every professional body appears to hold it is forwarding education, or perhaps rather satisfying its self-respect and rising to its position, by instituting schemes of examinations and insisting on these particular tests as alone valid. (MacLeod, 1982, p. 7)

A notable example amongst the professions was the medical profession (Mansell, 1982). A General Council of Medical Education and Registration was established by act of parliament in 1858, and in 1860 London University established a Preliminary Scientific Examination for medical students composed of six three hour written papers across all the sciences, and an oral and practical examination in chemistry. These reflected a determination in the university to emphasise scientific learning as a basis for medical training. As the examination evolved over the next thirty years, the practical laboratory components were enhanced.

However, the pass rates were only about 55 per cent, a situation which led to tensions between the scientists who set these examinations and the medical schools who were anxious to preserve their long-established and more empirical mode of training. Alternative routes were promoted, strongly resisted by the scientists who did not want to lose the students who formed a large proportion of their intake, but did not want either to be seen to lower their standards. The disputes that arose centred in part on a deep difference between the doctors, whose priority lay in a professional model of practical training for medicine, and the scientists who argued for a better theoretical basis. This was a typical case of examinations becoming a focus around which a fundamental debate about learning arose and raged. However, it is also the case that these examinations did raise the standards of entry to professional medical education.

One more effect followed. Whilst at first the schools could not teach to the standards required in the new examination, by the 1890s many were doing so. In this instance, as in others, the requirements of a profession affected the work of schools. The examinations were the means by which the 'gatekeepers' to a profession exercised their power, and this power filtered down to affect those anxious to provide their students with means of access.

Similar stories are set out in MacLeod's book about the examinations in science set up to control access to the academies of the military profession, for the civil service, for accountants and for solicitors. New examinations in technology were conducted by the City and Guilds Institute which was set up for this purpose by the craft guilds of the City of London in 1878. There were other initiatives of this type — for example, at a lower level for the training of artisans.

Friend or Foe?

The Universities

The universities were as deeply involved as any in the new testing culture. The first written examination was introduced in Oxford in 1702 and in Cambridge in 1800, but general abandonment of oral in favour of written tests became widespread only after 1830. A bishop, writing in 1855 about the new examinations in Cambridge expressed the mood of many:

> The wonderful effect of these institutions (i.e. examinations) in exciting industry and emulation among the young men and exalting the character of the College, are such as may even have surpassed the hope of their promoters. (MacLeod, 1982, p. 7)

Here, as in the professions, examinations were seen as an agent to raise standards, in part by motivating students to work hard. However, some reservations arose to temper the new enthusiasms. A typical expression of the negative reaction to the dominance of the new examinations was expressed by a leading scientist, T.H. Huxley, writing in 1895:

> at the end of three years (the student) was set down to a table and questioned pell-mell upon all the different matters with which he had been striving to make acquaintance. A worse system and one more calculated to obstruct the acquisition of sound knowledge and to give full pay to the 'crammer' and the 'grinder' could hardly have been devised by human ingenuity. (MacLeod, 1982, p. 10)

The examinations exercised their control of access, both for entry to the universities and for careers on graduation. A Cambridge biology don, reflecting on his experience at that time, wrote:

> As a boy in Cambridge I learnt that if a man got a first class he might be happy; if he got a second class he would be unhappy; and if he got a third class, nothing but misery and a colonial life awaited him. (MacLeod and Moseley, 1982, p. 203)

Thus, university examinations came to be seen as a necessary evil, their bad effects on learning being acknowledged by many who also judged that the universities, in the new situation of growing demand for entry and the need to reassure the public of their standards, could not do without them.

The Effects Upon Schools

The most significant effect of the universities' commitment to examinations was the influence that they came to exert on schools (Brock, 1982). The

University of London's matriculation examination, established in 1838, came to be a school leaving examination. Oxford and Cambridge moved in the 1850s from a system of screening examinations set for those already admitted to setting examinations for those at school. The first such examinations, the Oxford Locals, were initially seen as an extension of the university's work and not as a part of school education; candidates were entered by their parents. For a time, two types of examination were conducted, one using the university's own test papers, the others set on the school's own syllabus, marked by the candidates' own teachers and then checked by the university.

A critical point in the evolution of the system came when plans for a government Examination Council led the leading public schools to look to Oxford and Cambridge for protection, and so to the setting up of a new joint board by the two universities to provide a more systematic authentication of the work in the sixth forms of schools. It is notable that the system started as a dual one. Whilst certificates were awarded on the basis of written examinations and oral examinations conducted by university examiners, a school could also choose to be examined by visiting academics from the universities who would examine the internal work of the pupils and report to the school and to the university.

As in the case of the university examinations, there were negative reactions as these external examinations came to dominate school work. One of the leading figures in the development of school science education, H.E. Armstrong, wrote in 1897:

> However valuable examinations may be as a means of 'putting on the screw' on both teachers and taught, it is impossible to overrate the injury done under our present system by unduly 'forcing the pace' and neglecting the apparently unpromising material on behalf of those whose work is more likely to afford 'results'. The undue encouragement given to 'literary' methods, owing to the extreme difficulty of properly examining practically, is one of the greatest evils the system entails; the interference with freedom of action in schools, and the consequent check on the development of methods of training is another; and further confusion is introduced in consequence of an entire absence of co-ordination in the requirements of the different examining bodies. (Brock, 1982, p. 180)

Subsequent to this complaint, practical examinations in the sciences were introduced by the Oxford and Cambridge Board.

The 'absence of co-ordination' arose in part from the fact that the examinations which the universities were setting had come to serve two purposes — the provision of the school leaving certificates and control of access to the universities. It also arose because the different professions and their agencies, operating their own examination systems, were exerting independent pressures on schools.

National Control of Schools

All of the above discussion relates to effects on the secondary schools, schools which had been set up and supported by a variety of private bodies for the education of the middle classes. Elementary education for the working classes depended on government, and grants for such education were first offered in 1833. As demand rose, the cost rose also and calls for assurances of quality and safeguards against waste had to be heeded. So in 1862, the minister responsible, Robert Lowe, set up the notorious system of 'payment by results'. Age-related tests in reading writing and arithmetic were set and administered by the established national inspectors, who were thereby changed from being helpers of schools to being their inquisitors. The results were graphically described by one of these inspectors, writing in 1911, almost twenty years after the system had been abandoned:

> Not a thought was given, except in a small minority of the schools, to the real training of the child, to the fostering of his mental (and other) growth. To get him through the yearly examination by hook or by crook was the one concern of the teacher. As profound distrust of the teacher was the basis of the policy of the Department, so profound distrust of the child was the basis of the policy of the teachers. To leave the child to find anything out for himself, to work out anything for himself, to think out anything for himself, would have been regarded as proof of incapacity, not to say insanity, on the part of the teacher, and would have led to results which, from the 'percentage' point of view, would probably have been disastrous. (Holmes, 1911, pp. 107–8)

The system became increasingly difficult to control and audit as numbers grew further and as attempts were made to include in it a wider range of subjects. Its abandonment after thirty years owed more to the Treasury and the national audits than to any educational considerations (Sutherland, 1996; Broadfoot, 1996, pp. 200–4).

A parallel use of payment by results affected one area of teaching in the secondary schools. The Department of Science and Art (DSA), a private body set up after the Great Exhibition of 1851, was trying to stimulate the teaching of science and industrial art by offering incentives, via an examination system, to set up science or art classes. Teachers entering students for their examinations received 'payment by results'. The DSA also provided equipment grants, set up museum services and ran in-service courses for teachers. The examiners included several Fellows of the Royal Society. In 1899 the DSA became part of the government Board of Education, and the 1902 Education Act placed all responsibility for educational provision — but not for examining — in the hands of local education authorities, thereby rationalizing the previous complex system in which, local school boards, the DSA and local authorities had all played a part in organizing and supporting schools. The DSA episode was significant in that it was an example of a private body using examinations not to control, but to stimulate the development of science education. The resources it used went mainly to the working classes and T.H. Huxley called it 'the greatest engine yet invented for forcing science into ordinary education' (Coleman and Mansell, 1995, p. 151).

On this foundation, the public examination system developed in England. The universities, through the examination boards which they controlled, developed the school leaving examinations. The government set up a Secondary Schools Examination Council in 1917 to co-ordinate their work and under their auspices the School Certificate and Higher School Certificate examinations run by the boards became the main examinations at ages 16 and 18 (Montgomery, 1965). The characteristics which marked its development were reflected in the ways in which it became institutionalized. Political control was kept at arms length, and the universities became the dominant influence. By contrast, in Scotland, Wales and Northern Ireland, the public examinations were closely linked to the regional and local governments.

One disturbance arose in the 1930s when research studies were mounted to check some important aspects of the examining process (Hartog and Rhodes, 1936). The studies revealed that there could be large discrepancies between the marking of the same work by different examiners, and both the reliability and the validity of the results produced by the system were called into question. However, these disturbing results made no radical impact on the system.

The techniques of examining developed rather little over the first half of the twentieth century, there being strong reliance on written test papers with emphasis on essay writing and on remembered knowledge. In mathematics and the sciences, there was also emphasis on solution of problems which were in the main predictable in character so that, through intensive preparation, their solution owed more to hard work and routine than to originality and insight.

Intelligence Testing

A different influence arose from the development of the beliefs in genetic inheritance and the Darwinian principle of natural selection. Francis Galton argued in 1869 that human intelligence is largely a matter of genetic inheritance and this led him to set out 'scientific' programmes for the measurement of human beings. Such assumptions gained more practical power through the development of intelligence tests by the French psychologist, Alfred Binet, whose expertise as a psychologist was first recruited in 1905 by the French government to help select pupils in order to use educational resources most efficiently. The tests he produced were meant to be scientific, being designed to produce reliable results by using many short test items. These tests were in principle radically different from previous written examinations. The conventional tests gave a measure of attainment on programmes of learning already completed, and that attainment would be dependent on the many and varied learning experiences of the candidates as well as on their ability to benefit from those experiences. The intelligence test was seen as a predictor of cognitive potential, independent of the accidents of previous experience. Underlying such claims was the assumption that everyone has an innate intelligence determined in their genes.

In England, tests of this type were developed to ensure early identification of children with special educational needs, and were therefore used in the main with children of primary school age. The IQ and similar tests were 'standardized' by being tested against a broad cross-section of children over a range of ages, so that an IQ test, for example, would produce a score of 100 for a child who was at the average level of 'intelligence' of his or her age group. A child who achieved a score of only 70 might be automatically placed in a special school — although the fixing of the borderline, in this case at 70, might well be determined by the number of special school places available.

Overall, there grew up a tradition of 'scientific' standardized tests which were widely used by local government authorities in their schools, for diagnostic and selection purposes. Local education authorities had been conducting tests at age 11 to select for, and award scholarships for, secondary education since the early 1900s. The '11-plus' examinations used after 1945 to select the minority allowed to go from primary schools to the academic schools, used a mixture of standardized and more conventional tests. Whilst much controversy was aroused about the negative effects of the social selection which this examination produced, it was often a technically better, and a better researched, examination than the school leaving certificate tests in operation at that time. In general, however, the standardized tests bore little relation to the school curriculum. Because they were operated for different purposes and by different agencies from the public examination bodies, the two systems of testing, the one for selection and diagnosis pre-16 and the other for certification at and after 16 operated in almost total isolation from each other.

Evolving Systems

As mass education at secondary level developed from the 1950s, and the educational requirements for employment were raised through technological advance, pressures arose to provide school leaving certification through examinations for all pupils. The university-led school leaving examinations could not meet this need, being designed to select an academic elite from amongst the top 20 to 40 per cent of the school population. New examining authorities were set up on a regional basis under the control of groups of local authorities. They were to supplement the academic examinations for the General Certificate of Education, run by the traditional independent boards, with examination systems attuned to the needs of the broad majority of students. These examination systems bore some of the characteristics of the original university work with schools, emphasizing the schools' role in examining, and calibrating assessments made by teachers to supplement the results of external examinations. However, the new boards also enhanced teacher representation in the bodies that controlled both their curriculum and their assessment policies.

Through this new qualification, the Certificate of Secondary Education, new methods of school-based assessment were developed along with new methods to 'moderate' teachers' assessments to ensure that all schools were using common procedures and working to shared standards. These developments were also taken up in part by the GCE boards — at least one developed an experimental system in the 1960s which enabled pupils to gain a GCE in English entirely on the basis of teacher assessment with no external written examination. New influences were also beginning to broaden the range of techniques used in the public examinations. In the 1960s multiple choice questions were introduced in many examinations, in most cases through the influence of their widespread use in the USA. There were also new experiments in the use of a broader range of both written and practical examinations, and incorporation in public examinations of assessments by teachers of practical science, art and other constructive work became common.

Much of this research and innovation came to a focus in 1988 when, after about 18 years of planning, experimentation, and oft-deferred decisions, the dual system of GCE and CSE examinations was replaced by a single examination, the General Certificate of Secondary Education (Nuttall, 1990). The requirement of this examination, to discriminate amongst pupils over the whole range of school attainment, raised new technical problems, often solved by setting alternative, and in some sense overlapping papers attuned to different groups. Indeed, the new structure was called a 'Single System of Examinations at 16 plus' rather than a single examination to emphasize this feature. The examination was also characterized by the widespread incorporation of moderated teacher assessment in most subjects, covering those important aspects which by their nature could not be assessed by external written tests.

Whilst the new GCSE system required amalgamations between the former GCE and CSE boards, there was a high degree of continuity between the new system and the traditions and techniques of the former boards. At the same time the former GCE boards maintained their independent work with the examinations for A-level designed for the most academically successful pupils as a selection instrument for higher education. However, in the new system and in subsequent developments, government control over all aspects of this public examination system became more and more powerful, so that, for example, in 1992 the Prime Minister could decree that teacher assessments were making too large a contribution to the GCSE results so that this contribution had to be cut back, to centrally specified limits, by all of the new examining groups.

The 1988 Education Reform Act gave government new powers to set up national assessment at ages 7, 11 and 14 to be applied to all pupils in maintained schools. Central government had already embarked on a system of monitoring the performance of schools as a whole through the setting up of its Assessment of Performance Unit which had produced national sampling surveys in English, mathematics and science and, on a smaller scale, in modern foreign languages and design and technology, in the early 1980s. The groups contracted to do this work had to develop new assessment methods and new techniques of analysis and their work influenced both the day to day assessments in schools and the work of the GCSE groups. However, this work was brought to an end with the onset of national assessment.

The national assessment system again created the need for new developments in assessments. At first, under the original plans, the assessments were intended to be made by new types of assessment tasks requiring extensive involvement of teachers in methods intended to produce, particularly for primary pupils, test contexts which would be rather similar in style to their normal classroom. These ran into difficulties, and their initial problems were used, by those who wanted a more traditional type of testing, to argue for their abandonment. This reaction has been sustained, so that the national assessment has come to use mainly traditional written test methods of the type originally derived for age 16, whilst leaving the assessment of practical and performance achievements to un-calibrated teacher assessment.

Five Systems

The overall outcome is that in 1996 there are in England five parallel systems of testing and assessment. Firstly, there is the use of standardized tests for diagnostic and selection purposes, operated by local authorities and schools using instruments mainly developed by private commercial agencies.

Secondly, there are the national assessments at 7, 11 and 14, mainly operated under contract by units within the public examination groups. These use quite different techniques from the first group, but are close to the third group, which is constituted by the GCSE and GCE bodies, whose techniques and methods have evolved, but without radical discontinuity, from those of the late nineteenth century.

A fourth group includes all those concerned with vocational and occupational selection. Whilst these had spawned a vast array of testing procedures, the work of the several independent agencies working in this field, two of them with origins in the nineteenth century, has been rationalized by a government agency, the National Council for Vocational Qualifications. The tradition of assessment developed in this sector has been distinctive. The emphasis has been on assessment by the organization conducting the teaching or training. The function of the central body has been to set general guidelines and to license the teaching organizations so that their assessments have a seal of approval. This arises partly form the need for vocational assessment to be practical and in the working environment rather than academic and in the artificial context of examination rooms. The examination traditions represented by National Vocational Qualifications (NVQs) are spreading in schools and are clearly seen as providing quite different assessment routines and quite different motivation for pupils (Wolf, 1995).

The fifth area is informal — it is the area of the day-to-day assessment of the learning of their pupils by teachers in schools. Being largely private, this area has a thinly chronicled history even though its importance in securing high standards of learning is evident. Whilst its needs and possibilities are distinct, it has been very strongly driven by the influences of the other four areas: this issue will receive detailed attention in Chapter 7.

Assessment and Testing in the USA

Driven by Social Change

The developments in nineteenth century America began to follow the same path as in England. For example, Harvard introduced its first internal written examinations in 1833 and its first written entrance examinations in 1851. Written examinations for the government funded schools were introduced in Boston in 1845. As in England, the movement from rural to urban communities and the growth of an industrial economy created new demands on education. As long as the young in a village could follow traditional occupations for which they learnt 'on the job', school education was a disposable luxury and certification of achievement was unnecessary. Industrialization led to larger organizations with gradually increasing demands in literacy and numeracy and fewer posts for the uneducated. The recruits for their workforce came from large and shifting populations so that personal recommendation and patronage were no longer practicable as means for selection.

Added to this in the USA however was the huge tide of immigration in the 1920s and 1930s. The society had to absorb, educate and put to work newcomers from many countries and from many different cultures. In order to create and maintain a common national identity, there had to be some standardization in education. This need called for 'objective' and 'scientific' ways of testing, using methods for selection which would be fair to children coming from many different backgrounds.

The Growth of Standardized Testing

Binet's intelligence tests had been taken up by a psychologist — Lewis Terman at Stanford University — who developed, in 1916, the Stanford-Binet IQ test which has been the model for IQ tests ever since. However, he and others argued for the use of such tests with the general population and not just for those with learning disabilities. By this means, science could be used to organize education, and consequently employment in society, on a rational basis. The opportunity and resources to develop this dream came in the first world war when psychologists convinced the US army of the advantages of a programme of intelligence testing for all recruits. To carry through such a programme, the expensive one-on-one application of the IQ test had to be replaced. The multiple-choice test, first invented in 1915, provided the solution and a multiple-choice version of the Stanford-Binet test ushered in a new era in measurement. The use of the new test in the army established a body of data on 1.75 million people. This was a new era because through this development the IQ test was transformed from an instrument used by specialists to deal with a retarded minority to a means to make decisions about the future education and careers of normal people.

The multiple-choice test, derived from the tradition of intelligence testing, and further justified by the prevailing emphasis on managing learning through specification of behavioural objectives, provided an economical and defensible way of meeting the social needs of an expanding society. The overall population of the USA had risen by 69 per cent between 1890 and 1918 and the numbers of high school students had increased by over 700 per cent over the same period. A central system for college entrance examinations had already been set up when the College Entrance Examinations Board was established in 1900. After 1918, this board started to develop the use of multiple-choice tests with the aim of measuring aptitude in ways which were less dependent on the quality of the schools which applicants had attended. The multiple-choice Scholastic Aptitude Test was designed in the 1920s. It slowly gained precedence over the established essay tests, and in turbulence created by the second world war in the 1940s the essay tests disappeared and college entrance came to depend on a combination of the SAT plus short achievement tests — the whole in multiple-choice format and taken in a single day.

Set and marked from outside the schools, such tests could claim to be objective. Agencies grew up to construct and market tests to the states and to schools, and they developed a high level of technical expertise to serve their specific objectives. Achievement was to be quantified by the psychometricians, who developed their own vocabulary and their own professional mystique. The standardized and centralized tests that evolved gradually came to be used as the means to allot scholarships, as the instruments to determine access to employment and to higher education, and as the means used by the state governments to test the efficiency of their schools — even to the extent, in some states, of determining the funding the schools might receive. In consequence, one commentary has concluded that

> ... American students are the most frequently tested and least often examined students in the world. (Resnick and Resnick, 1985)

In many cases, the actual tests used were confidential, so that teachers and students would not know exactly what was being tested. The tests were not connected closely to any particular curriculum and so did not test the schools' learning work directly. Given these features, and the growth of the expert mystique, the testing was gradually separated from teaching. Thus, a movement which began as a means to help schools cope with their new problems, had transformed by the 1960s and 1970s into the provider of measures of educational excellence through which schools were controlled, by local and state governments and by higher education. It has been estimated that the number of standardized tests now administered annually in the USA is between 140 million and 400 million (Madaus and Raczek, 1996). The movement developed further with the establishment of regular sample survey tests conducted by the National Assessment of Educational Progress (NAEP) in the 1980s. These started with a stated intention to produce only a nationwide picture, then later developed to produce data for the performance of each state. This has been followed by talk of enhancing sampling to produce measures of each school district, and there was some consideration in the early 1990s of instituting blanket testing, i.e. tests of every individual pupil at particular ages. This last possibility was embraced by President Clinton in his 1996 State of the Union message, with a declared intention to make available for all a reading test (for age 8) and a mathematics test (for age 12).

The Reaction Against Multiple Choice

This dominance of multiple-choice testing is now under attack. Criticisms became prominent in the late 1960s, notably with the publication by Banesh Hoffmann (1962) of *The Tyranny of Testing*. The tests led pupils and teachers to think of learning as the art of picking the right answer. This reduced knowledge to the banal level of a set of right answers, attached to a set of many short questions which reflected an atomization of knowledge into numerous small and disconnected parts. Those activities which would be more constructive, creative and holistic, were not tested. Thus, because the particular test method could only sample a narrow range of types of performance, and because the tests were not linked to schedules of curriculum or instruction, critics argued that these tests could not be instruments to improve education. All they could do was to exert pressure on teachers to drill students to pick right answers, an orientation which was said to be inimical to good learning. At the same time, their value to employers and to higher education was called into question because they were too crude an instrument. In particular, as colleges tried to expand the numbers admitted, the standard test results became increasingly unsuitable to discriminate amongst a broader range of the population.

The strongest criticisms arose from the growing body of research into effective learning (Gifford and O'Connor, 1992). Here, the evidence indicated that learning is a complex process which cannot be reduced to a routine of selection of small components. Indeed, it was becoming clear that each learner has to construct her own schemes of understanding and that new knowledge has to be developed within the broad context of each learner's scheme. This tension between learning and some types of testing will be discussed further in Chapter 4.

These criticisms have been influential. In 1989, the tests of one of the standardized college entrance agencies, the American College Testing Assessment (ACT), were redesigned to enhance emphasis on conceptual and abstract thinking at the expense of factual recall, and the SAT was later redesigned in the same general way. There has arisen a broader wave of new developments in assessment, using a variety of new techniques, some borrowed from the traditional means established in England and in other countries. It is not clear, however, how these are to be used within reconstructed assessment and testing systems. The development is under pressure because of the difficulties of achieving objectivity and of satisfying other criteria of reliability at modest cost. For all their faults, multiple-choice methods do what they can do very cheaply.

Other sources of concern have arisen in the different area of the testing of young pupils (at ages 5 to 9) in order to determine their need for special education. Whilst such tests were designed to help pupils receive the special help to which they should be entitled, those who have studied the outcomes of selection now express concern that short standardized tests are not an effective way to determine the needs, so that it is estimated that about 40 per cent of the children tested are not being correctly diagnosed. In addition, the tests are not linked to the aims of the special education classes to which the children that they serve to select are sent; thus there is a mis-match between diagnosis and provision (Shepard and Graue, 1993).

Conclusion

This chapter has provided only some selective sketches of episodes in the development of testing and assessment. The contrast between the USA and England is probably more sharp than that between England and many other countries. One main difference across European countries is between those who place high reliance on oral examinations (particularly in higher education and notably in Eastern Europe) and those who make no use of them except to test oral communication as such. Another difference is between countries who have no external examinations, or use them lightly to help calibrate the schools who are entrusted with the main task of pupil certification, and those, like England, where such trust and the wholesale delegation of authority to schools which goes with it is politically unacceptable (See Chapter 9 for further discussion).

It is hard, from the perspective of English schools, to understand a system where there are no external tests which sample across the range of content and aims of the subjects they teach, and yet where there are high stakes multiple-choice tests on the basis of which schools will be judged and funded.

But it is equally hard, from the perspective of USA schools, to understand a system in which the whole span of their work with pupils is tested in national examinations for which national norm scores are hard to find and for which the reliability is nowhere expressed in quantitative terms.

That which is taken for granted in one context can be puzzling, even unthinkable, in another. There are no simple reasons for these differences. They are the product of national traditions, broad social forces, and perhaps the historical accidents of the growth of institutions with a stake in maintaining the particular methods and procedures to which they are attached or on which they depend.

What this account should serve to show is that many of the tensions and disagreements about testing and assessment which beset many of us now are not new. They can find echoes in the writings of over a century. Nevertheless, the contexts within which they now arise are new, the basis on which their seriousness may be judged is continually altered by research results, and the techniques available for tackling them are evolving all the time.

It should also serve to underline the comment by MacLeod (1982) that examinations are:

> . . . possibly the single most intrusive and expensive innovation in Western education in the last century. (p. 16)

Summary

- Tests were instituted in many societies to meet the need for selection into specialist or privileged occupations.
- The importance and nature of their function changes as societies evolve, from serving education for a small elite, through working with the larger numbers and wider aspirations of a middle class, to dealing with the needs and problems of education for all.

- There is also a common evolution, from diverse tests controlled by particular groups to serve their own interests, to tests controlled centrally by agencies serving a wide range of interests, usually controlled or influenced by politicians.
- Testing and assessment have evolved also through the development of new methods in response to the technical challenges posed by social changes.
- There is a basic difference between tests which claim to measure underlying traits, or aptitudes, or potential — and so claim also to be unaffected by teaching and learning work — and those which claim to measure the success of those who have studied in particular learning programmes.
- Testing and assessment interact with learning; the interaction can be a forward one, in the composition of testing regimes to reflect and support learning aims, or a backward one by the influence of high stakes tests on the goals and methods of work of both teachers and students.
- The assessment and testing systems within any given society can only be understood in relation to the history and culture of its educational and social systems.

Bibliography

BROADFOOT, P.M. (1996) *Education, Assessment and Society. A Sociological Analysis*, Buckingham: Open University Press. Chapter 4 discusses the emergence of the concept of assessment in terms of modern sociological theories.

GIPPS, C. and STOBART, G. (1993) *Assessment: A Teachers' Guide to the Issues*, London: Hodder and Stoughton. Chapters 1, 7 and 8.

HANSON, F.A. (1993) *Testing Testing: Social Consequences of the Examined Life*, Berkeley and Los Angeles CA: University of California Press. Chapter 7 for USA history. The book as a whole covers a broad range to include such issues as drug testing and so-called lie detectors.

MacLEOD, R. (ed.) (1982) *Days of Judgement: Science, Examinations and the Organisation of Knowledge in Late Victorian England*, Driffield: Nafferton Books. Particularly Introduction and Chapters 4, 7 and 9.

STIGGINS, R.J. (1994) *Student-Centered Classroom Assessment*, New York: Merrill/Macmillan. Chapter 2 for USA perspective.

WOOD, R. (1991) *Assessment and Testing*, Cambridge: Cambridge University Press. Chapter 7.

References

BROADFOOT, P.M. (1996) *Education, Assessment and Society: A Sociological Analysis*, Buckingham: Open University Press.

BROADFOOT, P.M., MURPHY, R. and TORRANCE, H. (eds) (1990) *Changing Educational Assessment: International Perspectives and Trends*, London: Routledge.

BROCK, W.H. (1982) 'School science examinations: Sacrifice or stimulus?', in MACLEOD, R. (ed.) *Days of Judgement: Science, Examinations and the Organization of Knowledge in Late Victorian England*, Driffield: Nafferton Books, pp. 169–88.

COLEMAN, D. and MANSELL, T. (1995) 'Science religion and the School Board: Aspects of the life and work of John Hall Gladstone', *History of Education*, **24**, pp. 141–58.

GIFFORD, B.R. and O'CONNOR, M.C. (eds) (1992) *Changing Assessments: Alternative Views of Aptitude, Achievement and Instruction*, Boston and Dordrecht; Kluwer.

GOLDSTEIN, H. and LEWIS, T. (eds) (1996) *Assessment: Problems, Development and Statistical Issues*, Chichester and New York: John Wiley.

HANSON, F.A. (1993) *Testing Testing: Social Consequences of the Examined Life*, Berkeley and Los Angeles: University of California Press.

HARTOG, P. and RHODES, E.C. (1936) *The Marks of Examiners*, London: Macmillan.

HOFFMANN, B. (1962) *The Tyranny of Testing*, New York: Crowell-Collier.

HOLMES, E. (1911) *What Is and What Might Be*, London: Constable, pp. 107–8.

MACLEOD, R. (ed.) (1982) *Days of Judgement: Science, Examinations and the Organization of Knowledge in Late Victorian England*, Driffield: Nafferton Books.

MACLEOD, R. and MOSELEY, R. (1982) 'Breaking the circle of the sciences: The natural sciences tripos and the "examination revolution"', in MACLEOD, R. (ed.) *Days of Judgement: Science, Examinations and the Organization of Knowledge in Late Victorian England*, Driffield: Nafferton Books, pp. 189–212.

MADAUS, G.F. and RACZEK, A.E. (1996) 'The extent and growth of educational testing in the United States 1956–1994', in GOLDSTEIN, H. and LEWIS, T. (eds) *Assessment: Problems, Developments and Statistical Issues*, Chichester and New York: John Wiley, pp. 145–65.

MANSELL, A.L. (1982) 'Examination and medical education: The preliminary sciences in the examinations of the London University and the English Conjoint Board, 1861–1911', in MACLEOD, R. (ed.) *Days of Judgement: Science, Examinations and the Organization of Knowledge in Late Victorian England*, Driffield: Nafferton Books, pp. 87–107.

MONTGOMERY, R.J. (1965) *Examinations: An Account of their Evolution as Administrative Devices in England*, London: Longman.

NUTTALL, D.L. (1990) 'The GCSE: Promise versus reality', in BROADFOOT, P.M., MURPHY, R. and TORRANCE, H. (eds) *Changing Educational Assessment: International Perspectives and Trends*, London: Routledge, pp. 143–8.

RESNICK, D.P. and RESNICK, L.B. (1985) 'Standards, curriculum and performance: A historical and comparative perspective', *Educational Researcher*, **14**, pp. 5–20.

SHEPARD, L.A. and GRAUE, M.E. (1993) 'The morass of school readiness screening: Research on test use and test validity', pp. 293–305 in SPODEK, B. (ed.) *Handbook of Research on the Education of Young Children*, New York: Macmillan.

SPODEK, B. (ed.) (1993) *Handbook of Research on the Education of Young Children*, New York: Macmillan.

SUTHERLAND, G. (1996) 'Assessment: Some historical perspectives', pp. 9–20 in GOLDSTEIN, H. and LEWIS, T. (eds) *Assessment: Problems, Developments and Statistical Issues*, Chichester and New York: John Wiley.

WOLF, A. (1995) *Competence Based Assessment*, Buckingham: Open University Press.

Chapter 3

Purposes

Introduction

Assessments may be conducted to serve several different purposes. In this chapter, the main types of purpose will be discussed in three main sections, concerned respectively with the support of learning, with reporting the achievements of individuals, and with satisfying demands for public accountability. These three sections will be followed by consideration of the interactions, supportive or conflicting, between these purposes.

It is important to match the selection and use of assessment methods to the particular purpose which the assessment is meant to serve and a distinction has to be made at the outset between the purposes and the instruments and procedures that might be used. For example, the same test questions may be used for quite different purposes, and, conversely, a single purpose might be served by combining the results obtained from a range of different types of assessment. Furthermore, assessments may be carried out by many different agencies, from the teacher in the classroom to a committee mounting an international survey. Issues concerning the choices of assessment methods and the locus of responsibility for planning and administering assessments will be taken up in later chapters.

Support of Learning

Formative Assessment

The importance of this function is expressed in the following passage from a USA author:

> ... the teacher has need of constant information about what the student knows and the strategies being used to process and comprehend new concepts ... By imbedding diagnostic instruction in instructional activities, teachers can preserve the integrity of assessment tasks (the wholeness of tasks and natural learning context) and protect instructional time that would otherwise be diverted to testing ... There is general agreement that external packaged tests will not solve the problem of what teachers need to know about student learning. (Shepard, 1992)

The issue is also emphasized, in a different way, in the following extract, already introduced in Chapter 1, from the TGAT report:

> Promoting children's learning is a principal aim of schools. Assessment lies at the heart of this process. It can provide a framework in which educational objectives may be set, and pupils' progress charted and expressed. It can yield a basis for planning the next educational steps in response to children's needs. By facilitating dialogue between teachers, it can enhance professional skills and help the school as a whole to strengthen learning across the curriculum and throughout its age range. (DES, 1988)

Taken together, these extracts cover a number of different points about the uses of assessment to improve learning. Outstanding is the principle that feedback is essential to the conduct of effective teaching. No system, mechanical or social, can adjust and adapt as it performs its task without that frequent information about the operation of its system which is needed to modify the input in the light of the actual — rather than the intended or imagined — progress of the system. This is particularly important in any enterprise where the response may be very variable and unpredictable — which is surely true of most classrooms.

Effective teaching ought to vary in pace and style according to the needs of the learners. Teachers need to go slowly, or repeat what has been done, when difficulties of their pupils become apparent. They need also to differentiate their teaching as they collect evidence that some have grasped ideas and want to go ahead, whereas others are trapped in confusions so that they are unable to go ahead. Whilst some differentiation may be achieved by setting, which can be a matter for controversy, all agree that even within a group chosen on the basis of a particular band of achievements, there will be a wide range of understandings and of rates of progress. Teachers need sound information on which to base differentiation decisions, and insofar as remedial action can be taken, its efficacy also needs to be checked. Individualized learning schemes are set up on the extreme view that pupils may be so different that each has to work at his or her own pace. However, the outstanding characteristic of such schemes is that assessment of attainment becomes the keystone in determining the progress of each pupil's learning work.

Ideally, assessment should provide short term feedback so that obstacles can be identified and tackled. This is particularly important where the learning plan is such that progress with this week's work depends on a grasp of the ideas discussed last week. Such assessment is generally called **formative**. It is clear that formative assessment is the responsibility of the classroom teacher, but others, in the school or outside, can support such work by providing training and methods.

All formative assessment is to a degree diagnostic, and the term **diagnostic** assessment is also used. Although it is hard to distinguish diagnostic from formative by dictionary definitions, in practice the two are used with different emphases, even though their ranges of application overlap. Standardized tests, constructed and refined by experts, are often used in a school to help identify special and extreme learning difficulties. The need here is for expert precision because the learning problems might be both deep and general, so that the type of adjustment that can be made on the spot in a normal classroom cannot possibly meet the special need. Such tests are said to be diagnostic. Thus, diagnostic assessment is an expert and detailed enquiry into underlying difficulties, and can lead to radical re-appraisal of a pupil's needs, whereas formative assessment is more superficial in assessing problems with particular classroom work, and can lead to short-term and local changes in the learning work of a pupil.

Curriculum, Pedagogy and the Formative Function

Because formative assessment is intended as the feedback needed to make learning adaptive and thereby more effective, it cannot simply be added as an extra to an existing, non-interactive, scheme of work. The feedback procedures, and more particularly their use in varying the teaching and learning programme, have to be built into the teaching plans, which thereby will become both more flexible and more complex. This is emphasized very strongly by Linn (1989):

> ... the design of tests useful for the instructional decisions made in the classroom requires an integration of testing and instruction. It also requires a clear conception of the curriculum, the goals, and the process of instruction. And it requires a theory of instruction and learning and a much better understanding of the cognitive processes of learners. (p. 5)

This quotation opens up further issues. The teacher has to decide what to assess, and to interpret the pupil's work in terms of a need that might require attention. In one topic, the fact that a pupil has not yet grasped a particular idea might not matter, in that it will be encountered again later and until then that grasp will not be needed. In another topic, a particular understanding may be an essential basis for work in the immediate future, so that the pupils will be disabled unless the present difficulty can be dealt with now. Judgments about what can be left and about what has to be grasped now are rarely clear cut. Thus, the practice of formative assessment has to be informed by a model that is quite detailed, in that it has to provide some guidance about the ways in which a pupil might progress in learning, linked to a clear conception of the curriculum and its learning goals. The reactions against multiple choice testing, discussed in Chapter 2, were in part driven by the realization that they could not give useful information in relationship to new models of learning.

A different issue is raised by the above quotation from the TGAT report in its use of the phrase 'by facilitating dialogue', which follows from the statement 'a framework in which . . . and pupils' progress charted and expressed', and which leads to hopes for strengthening the whole work of the school. The formulation of a policy about learning, and interaction between teachers and others about the framing and implementation of such policy, requires a language in which learning aims and achievements can be discussed. Such language must be linked to concrete examples, both of pupils' achievements and of teachers' actions in learning, for without this it will be merely abstract and idealistic with little practical effect. Formative assessment should provide those examples, develop this language, and enrich and so give meaning to the shared understanding of ideas and policies about learning.

All of these arguments should make clear that the improvement of formative assessment is a complex enterprise, yet one which should be at the heart of any policy which aims to improve pupils' learning, and which will also be at the heart of the enterprise of classroom teaching. It would be optimistic to assume that teachers usually have sound information about the progress of their pupils' learning — the evidence is that this is far from being the case. Many practical issues also arise, concerned with the collection, analysis, recording and interpretation of data for formative assessment and with the adaptations of classroom practice that may have to ensue. All of these issues will be discussed in more detail in Chapter 7.

Certification, Progress and Transfer

Summative Assessment Within a School

Whenever pupils move so that responsibility for their learning is transferred from one teacher to another, information should also be transferred so that the new teacher can plan work and guide each pupil appropriately. The information needed for this purpose will depend on how the work in the new class is related to the old. If there is close continuity, then the formative information about recent progress and immediate needs that the old teacher would have needed is also needed by the new.

However, the new teacher might also need an overview of each pupil's recent achievements and progress in order to be able to anticipate the progress and needs of each, which might affect the organization of the new classroom and the distribution of learning tasks. If the new work is very different from the old, for example if it involves a fresh start in which the subject is tackled afresh at a more sophisticated level than hitherto, then here again the information needed is more general — an overview of the pupil's earlier achievement which might help predict capacity to profit from the new learning programme.

Thus, on transfer the need for **summative** assessment arises. The term implies an overview of previous learning. This could be obtained by an accumulation of evidence collected over time, or by test procedures applied at the end of the previous phase which covered the whole area of the previous learning. Beneath the key phrases here, 'accumulation' or 'covered', lies the problem of selecting that information which is most relevant for the summative purpose. The principles of selection might depend on one's beliefs about what matters for the next phase of learning in the subject (and might therefore differ between different curriculum subjects) and might also depend on the particular transition that is involved.

As argued above, for transfer between classes in the same school, with a high degree of continuity, the difference between assessment for the formative purpose and for the summative might be rather small. Indeed, within the work of one year group, a teacher might gather formative evidence and supplement it with a comprehensive test in order to review and to decide on structural changes — for example to change the grouping of pupils. This might be seen as a weak form of summative assessment, happening quite frequently, and there would be a close link, and a difference of degree rather than of kind, between the teacher's formative and summative work.

However, transfer between different stages of schooling and between different teachers imposes new requirements. If it is to be an effective communication, the assessment information has to be formulated with a structure and a language that reflects a shared understanding between those who are communicating. It will not be enough that the two teachers communicating are working to a common scheme of work. It will be necessary also that the information satisfies three further criteria:

- It has to be adequately detailed. To say that a pupil has a grade C in science may convey little: a profile which showed any variations in this grade between (say) practical investigative work, learning of facts, and tackling of numerical problems would be far more useful.
- The two teachers have to be working to common criteria for grading. Given a report by a pupil on a practical investigation, one of the teachers might have given it a B and the other a D because they worked to different criteria — one teacher giving priority to orderly structure and clarity of expression in a report, the other to the quality of scientific thinking revealed in the investigation design and in the interpretation of the results.
- There should also be a shared procedure for determining standards of grading. Two teachers could be using the same criteria but have different standards for interpretation of the conventional grades in terms of marks — a decision by one to give (say) a B grade might be seen by the other as far too generous.

Transfer Between and Out of Schools

These problems are more difficult to overcome if a summative assessment is to help guide the transfer of pupils between institutions — for example, between primary and secondary school, or from secondary school to a sixth-form college. Communication of criteria and standards will be less informal, so more priority has to be given to clear and agreed documentation. In addition, for each of the examples mentioned, several different schools will be sending pupils to the same higher institution. Unless these schools are working to common schemes and produce assessments on a shared basis the summative assessment information will be worthless. Thus, either different schools have to cooperate closely and accept constraints on their freedom to work in their own ways, or curricula and assessment have to be formally established and operated by external agencies. This is one of many examples where each school's own desire for its freedom of manoeuvre has to be reconciled with constraints which can be justified by the broader needs of their pupils.

Transfer to a new type of school can place a pupil in a very different type of learning environment. It will then be more difficult to predict, on the basis of previous achievements, how that pupil will progress in the new school. Ideally, the success of primary schools in predicting secondary progress ought to be investigated by monitoring the secondary school progress, so that their summative assessments can be improved. A great deal of such analysis used to be carried out when an examination at 11 (the 'eleven-plus') was widely used in England and Wales to determine the type of secondary school to which a pupil was to be directed. This analysis was used to modify procedures for interpreting the test — and school assessment — data to maximize the efficiency of prediction.

Such considerations also bear on the large discontinuities involved when pupils move either out of school into employment, or to further and more advanced study, whether at ages 16, or 18, or on completion of an undergraduate degree course. Here there may be very little direct link between the learning work, which might be the subject for any assessment, and the future needs. The issue is further complicated because these future needs may be very diverse, ranging over various types and levels of further education and over many different types of employment. It is clearly almost impossible to imagine that a single grade can give information useful for all these purposes.

A set of grades obtained over several subjects may be a better guide. If, within each subject, the results were a profile reflecting success in meeting different types of demand, the user would have an even better chance of looking selectively at what was needed for his purpose. It might help to add to this information quite different assessments cutting across the boundaries of school subjects; possible assessments of so-called 'core skills' and assessments of personality characteristics are possible additions here. Overall, the need is for multi-dimensional data, but whilst such complexity can guard against simplistic judgments, it can also make demands on those using the information to study and understand its structure and its terminology, and also to keep up with the inevitable frequent changes.

Within this context, public examinations can be considered in relation to their function of certificating individuals. As will be discussed below, such examinations also have a function in judging teachers and schools for accountability purposes. In the UK, the national curriculum tests for ages 7, 11 and 14, the General Certificate for Secondary Education (GCSE); the Advanced-level (A-level), the National Vocational Qualifications (NVQ) and many others for older school pupils, and university degree examinations, are all in this category. These examinations are clearly summative, but they may also contribute to teachers' formative work, by helping each teacher to check standards and by providing good examples of assessment tasks. In principle, such certification systems can use teacher assessments as part of their evidence. In some countries, the responsibilities are left entirely in the hands of teachers, in others teachers' judgments play no part. In most countries, external and school based assessments are combined in a variety of ways — some of these will be discussed further in Chapter 9.

Overall Issues

The certification purpose of assessment raises three main issues:

- The assessment has to be as effective as possible in relation to its purpose. Here, the precise requirements can differ a great deal across this category — from transfer between infants and juniors at age 7 to the transition to employment of a university student on graduation. Each transfer requires its own methods, and what is generally lacking is research data, on the relationship between assessment results and subsequent attainments, which could be used to improve those methods.
- There have to be choices about who is to control the process and who is to carry it out. Here are included choices about the local or national control and about whether this control is general and flexible or close and detailed. Closely linked to such choices is the assignment of responsibility to teachers and schools, or to external agencies, or to a combination of these.
- Decisions have to take account of the costs implied. The cost of public examinations is a significant item in the budgets of secondary schools, and for all schools summative assessments which have to work to shared external standards bear a high cost in terms of the time of classroom teachers and of school managements.

Accountability

Accountability and Test Results

Schools have a responsibility to the public who fund them. One aspect of the discharge of that responsibility is to provide evidence that they are indeed promoting the learning of their pupils. An economical way to do this is to provide aggregation of the results of their pupils' performance in the various public examination systems which their pupils have to take for their own personal needs — i.e. those discussed in the previous section.

Assessment data will have to be detailed if they are to be a useful guide. However, such data on their own cannot provide valid guidance. A school working with pupils of poor educational background in an area of social deprivation where parental support is limited may be producing results which are below a national average but which, in the circumstances of that school, represent an outstanding achievement. Thus, data on the achievements on intake of the pupils, and on the catchment area and the pupils' home backgrounds, will also have to be considered in making any judgment or taking any action on assessment results. More generally, a wide range of data are needed if the achievements of the pupils in any one school are to be interpreted.

This is not to say that poor outcomes and real needs are to be hidden by some form of manipulation. Distinctions have to be made here — again in relation to the purpose for which the information is to be used. If the poor results of a school can be shown to be related to a low budget and to large class sizes, the policy guidance is that action has to be taken on the resource determinants. If the performance and careers of the teachers in that school are to be judged, then allowance has to be made in the light of the factors which constrain them. If a parent has to decide whether or not to send her child to that school, then the judgment involves different considerations again. An alternative school may produce much better results, but if it also has a vary favourable intake, it could be that for a given pupil of average attainment, that school may not do as well for that pupil as one which appears to have less impressive test results.

There has been much controversy about whether or not it is fair to publish school test results in 'league tables'. The justification that they can guide parental choice is a weak one, insofar as comparisons made without allowance for the many features which affect the results can be misleading and so lead to inappropriate choices. Many have argued that it would be fairer to schools and more helpful to parents to publish 'value-added' data, comparing intake test results with later attainments. However, a school's circumstances can affect its pupils' capacity to make progress as well as their starting points. Such complications will not be pursued further here — the general problems of judging school effectiveness raise issues beyond the scope of this book (see Gray, 1996).

Helping Schools to Improve

It may be natural to think of comparisons, but the public interest ought also to focus on whether certain agreed standards have been reached. Here the question of uniformity of assessments across schools becomes important. The detail and multidimensionality of reporting will also matter if the assessment is to indicate where the particular strengths and weaknesses of each school may lie. This last point raises the larger question of how those responsible for schools may act on the information about their work that assessment results may provide.

However, this question implies two assumptions. The first is that the assessment data are suitable for this purpose. For example, if a particular set of primary schools adjust their summative reporting to meet needs agreed with a particular secondary school, these reports may not be comparable with those in another district, even in the same urban area, so that comparisons cannot be made. Similarly, where the demands of local employment are quite specific, the adjustment of information to meet the needs of the local community may be in tension with a demand for uniform standards and for comparison with other schools.

Problems of interpreting results for policy purposes can arise within a school. Most secondary schools undertake careful examination of GCSE and A-level results. Such reviews can be helped by data on the average performances over the country in each particular subject and, where entry to a given subject examination is limited because it is a matter for optional choice, by comparisons of the general attainment of those pupils who enter for that particular subject. Because there can be quite marked differences between the entry groups for different subjects — some, for example, attracting the more capable, or repelling all but the most capable and committed, comparisons of performances between one subject and another have to be made with care, whether they are to apply at the level of school departments or nationally (see Fitzgibbon, 1996). Comparisons in relation to national assessment can be helped again by national data, both for test results as a whole and at the level of individual items. (Software for this purpose has been produced by the UK School Curriculum Assessment Authority).

Sampling Surveys

Another way in which assessments which might inform policy can differ from those for individual certification lies in the possibilities of sampling. To produce an overall picture of a nation's performance, it is not necessary to test every pupil within a given age group. The APU in the UK, for example, tested only about 2 per cent of each of three age groups. Moreover, even that gave sample sizes of about 12 000 for each test, whereas for any one set of questions it could be shown that a sample of about 500, if carefully distributed over different types of school and different regions, could give an adequately stable average. What was in fact done was to give about thirty different sets of questions to different selected sets of pupils. This made it possible for the surveys to explore a wider range of attainments in greater detail than would be possible with a test which would have to be the same for every pupil. In consequence, the data obtained were far richer, far more interesting and useful to teachers, and have been more relevant to policy debates than public examination data have ever been, or than the national assessment test data are proving to be (Black, 1990; Gipps and Stobart, 1993, pp. 34–36, 40–42). This approach, of giving different tests to different and restricted samples to enhance the value of the data, is known as **matrix light sampling**. It has been used in several countries, notably the USA, Australia and New Zealand, as well as in the UK's APU surveys. The issues here bear on the content and construct validity of assessment results — issues to be taken up in Chapter 4.

If the accountability to be secured is that of individual schools, it might still be possible to produce information that is less costly and more informative by giving different tests to different samples of pupils rather than by giving them all the same test. However, this could only be the case for large schools where any one age cohort would be large enough for the purpose.

Interactions Between Purposes

The choices which will distinguish or adapt assessments to their purposes may be made at several levels:

- At the outset, the particular set of test items or procedures may be chosen to fit to the purpose.
- Then the way in which these are administered and marked may differ according to the purpose.
- The ways in which the outcomes may be analysed or combined could also vary with the purpose.
- Finally, a particular purpose may require its own specific interpretation of that assessment data.

The three elements to be addressed here are assessment methods, assessment agencies and the purposes. One testing method carried out by a single agency might serve more than one purpose and would thereby be economical. If on the other hand, the methods to be used for different purposes have to be completely different, or the interests of different agencies are in tension or even opposed, then separation is required.

Certification with Accountability

One example is the possibility that tests given to all pupils for the certification purpose could provide all that is needed for the accountability purpose. Most of the arguments which bear on this possibility have been touched upon in the previous section in the discussion of sampling surveys. Sample surveys can provide better quality information at lower costs than the certification tests for every pupil, but if the certification test for all is a priority and has to be used, then the sampling survey comes as extra expense. The cost is not only financial. External assessments create work for teachers whilst making it more difficult for them to get on with their normal tasks. Thus, it was understandable, although regrettable, that with the coming of national testing for all at 7, 11, and 14 in the UK, the national surveys of the APU were discontinued in spite of the loss of the detailed information that the surveys alone could provide. Here it can be seen that the two purposes are in tension, so that to give priority to the one is to reduce a system's capacity to serve the other.

Formative with Summative

A second and more notable example is the possibility that assessment by teachers might serve both the formative and summative purposes for their pupils and so remove the need for operation of separate agencies and procedures to serve the certification purpose. Some have laid stress on the differences between the formative and summative purposes, and have argued that the assessment instruments and procedures needed for the one are so different from those for the other that neither can flourish without clear separation. On the other side, it can be argued that the two functions are two ends of the same spectrum and that there is no sharp difference, and that if the two functions are separated, then teachers' assessment work will be devalued. These arguments will be taken further in the section on *Two Roles in Tension* in Chapter 7.

Purposes in Tension?

More will be said about these tensions in later chapters, for they raise more extensive technical arguments, whilst also moving into issues which are matters of public and political priority. What should be clear is that, in this second example as in the first, the two purposes are in tension. The time and effort needed by teachers if they were to bear the whole of the certification role would be extensive and might make it harder for them to develop and implement improved formative assessment. On the other hand, where very important decisions are based on wholly external tests, both pupils and teachers have to direct their work to meet the narrow range of demands which economical external testing can provide — and the model of teachers' own assessment inevitably becomes one of using examples of the external tests to train pupils, thereby weakening teachers' own formative assessment practices.

Whilst some degree of tension is inevitable, there can also be synergy. Instruments developed and trialled carefully by experts for certification and accountability exercises can be used by teachers to enrich their own range of questions used for the formative work. The work a teacher might have to do with peers to ensure common external standards when contributing to a certification process directed by an outside agency might well help that teacher towards a better appreciation of the aims and standards to which she should be working in her own formative assessment.

Summary

- The three main purposes of assessment are
    - formative, to aid learning,
    - summative for review, transfer and certification, and
    - summative for accountability to the public.

- The practice of formative assessment must be closely integrated with curriculum and pedagogy and is central to good quality teaching.
- The formative and summative labels describe two ends of a spectrum of practice in school-based assessment rather than two isolated and completely different functions.
- There are different levels of summative activity; summing up may be needed:
    - during the progress of work in one class,
    - on transfer between classes in a school,
    - for transfer between two schools, or between school and employment or further and higher education.

- The results of assessment and testing for accountability should:
    - be related to common criteria and standards,
    - be linked with comprehensive and detailed data on the school's intake and context, for otherwise the data will be unfair and misleading,
    - be designed and communicated so that they can serve the improvement of schools.

- Sample surveys may be a more efficient way of informing policy for the improvement of learning than blanket testing of all pupils.

- There are tensions between the different purposes of assessment and testing, which are often difficult to resolve, and which involve choices of the best agencies to conduct assessments and of the optimum instruments and appropriate interpretations to serve each purpose.

Bibliography

AIRASIAN, P.W. (1991) *Classroom Assessment*, New York: McGraw Hill. Chapter 1.

GIPPS, C.V. (1994) *Beyond Testing: Towards a Theory of Educational Assessment*, London: Falmer. Chapter 3.

GIPPS, C. and STOBART, G. (1993) *Assessment. A Teachers' Guide to the Issues*, London: Hodder and Stoughton. Chapter 2.

SALVIA, J. and YSSELDYKE, J.E. (1991) *Assessment*, Boston: Houghton Mifflin. Chapter 1.

STIGGINS, R.J. (1994) *Student-Centered Classroom Assessment*, New York: Merrill/Macmillan. Chapters 3 and 4.

WOOD, R. (1991) *Assessment and Testing*, Cambridge: Cambridge University Press. Chapters 8 (diagnostic assessment), 17 (aptitude testing) and 18 (personnel selection and assessment).

References

BLACK, P.J. (1990) 'APU science — the past and the future', *School Science Review*, **72**, 258, pp. 13–28.

DEPARTMENT OF EDUCATION AND SCIENCE (DES) (1988) *National Curriculum: Task Group on Assessment and Testing: A Report*, London: Department of Education and Science.

FITZGIBBON, C.T. (1996) *Monitoring Education: Indicators, Quality and Effectiveness*, London: Cassell.

GIFFORD, B.R. and O'CONNOR, M.C. (eds) (1992) *Changing Assessments: Alternative Views of Aptitude, Achievement and Instruction*, Boston and Dordrecht: Kluwer.

GIPPS, C. and STOBART, G. (1993) *Assessment: A Teachers' Guide to the Issues*, London: Hodder and Stoughton.

GOLDSTEIN, H. and LEWIS, T. (eds) (1996) *Assessment: Problems, Developments and Statistical Issues*, Chichester and New York: John Wiley.

GRAY, J. (1996) 'The use of assessment to compare institutions', in GOLDSTEIN, H. and LEWIS, T. (eds) *Assessment: Problems, Developments and Statistical Issues*, Chichester and New York: John Wiley, pp. 121–33.

LINN, R.L. (1989) 'Current perspectives and future directions', in LINN, R.L. (ed.) *Educational Measurement*, 3rd edn., London: Collier Macmillan, pp. 1–10.

SHEPARD, L.A. (1992) 'Commentary: What policy makers who mandate tests should know about the new psychology of intellectual ability and learning', in GIFFORD, B.R. and O'CONNOR, M.C. (eds) *Changing Assessments: Alternative Views of Aptitude, Achievement and Instruction*, Boston and Dordrecht: Kluwer, pp. 301–28.

Chapter 4

Confidence in Assessment — Reliability and Validity

Confidence in the Result

The results of assessments are used for one or more purposes. So they have an effect on those who are assessed and on those who use the results. Some of the effects are small — a pupil may be told to repeat a piece of work. Some are very big — failure to obtain a particular A-level grade can mean that the candidate must abandon her hopes of becoming a doctor. Thus it matters, more or less, that the result is dependable, that the users of the results can have confidence in them.

Discussion of the problems affecting the confidence that can be placed in an assessment is usually split into two parts, one to do with reliability and the other to do with validity. These two are best seen as separate dimensions or perspectives of the same problem, which interact with one another. So this chapter starts with separate discussions of reliability and validity. However, testing also affects the ways in which teachers teach and pupils learn, so the section on validity is followed by and expanded in a discussion of this concept in relation to models of learning. The interactions between validity and reliability are then explored.

Different issues are raised by the many problems attendant on bias in testing. A section on this topic forms the last substantive section here; it is followed by some general conclusions and the summary.

Reliability

Threats to Reliability

Reliability is the more straightforward issue. A pupil takes a particular task, perhaps a particular set of questions, on a particular day. His efforts are marked by a particular examiner, the marks are checked and analysed, and then the results are interpreted in terms of a grade or level. So, for example, this pupil ends up with a grade C in GCSE history. The problem about such a result is expressed as follows by Wood (1991):

> Given an individual's performance on a particular task at a particular point in time assessed by a particular assessor, how **dependable** is the inference to how that individual would have performed across all occasions, tasks, observers and settings? (p. 43)

The inference which Wood describes is a generalization from the particular result, so that this problem is often described as a problem of generalizability. The various ways in which an individual's result might have come out differently may be summarized under two main headings — those to do with the examiners' judgments and those to do with variability in the pupils' responses.

Errors in Marking

- Errors in the addition and transfer of marks.
  This source can be all but eliminated by having independent checking procedures.
- A different examiner might have given different marks.

When only one examiner is involved, occasional and independent checks on that examiner's methods and judgments can be used. Where a team of examiners have to share out the task of marking a large number of answers, training is essential to ensure that they all understand and apply a common scheme of marking in the same way, and both statistical data and checks on samples of each examiner's work are also used to ensure comparability across examiners. Occasionally, for example, a GCSE board might scale an examiner's marks up or down if the statistics show that he has been careful but consistently too harsh or too lenient. If an examiner turns out to be inconsistent, all of his work may have to be re-marked by others. A statement from one of the examining boards sets out a clear position about the problems in this area:

> It will be sufficient here to point out that all boards which at present offer certificates based on external examinations have to take this problem very seriously if they are to maintain any credibility, and that it is probably true to say that none of them will ever completely solve it. (University of Cambridge Local Examinations Syndicate, 1976, p. 9)

The seriousness of the problems involved here is clear from the results of many research enquiries which have explored the extent to which different markers of written tests can agree when they mark independently. For essay questions, correlations between pairs of markers rarely exceed 0.6 (Wood, 1991, pp. 57–8).

- The examiner might be more lenient or more harsh than in previous years.

This source is hard to tackle. Examiners have to use their judgment to ensure that standards are comparable from one year to the next. There is less of a problem if tests are kept confidential so that the same questions are repeated, although the interpretation of the results may still change: it might be that, for a new curriculum, the preparation of pupils for the examination becomes more efficient from one year to the next, so that a particular pupil may have done better if she had been prepared for the examination a year later.

Variations in Grading

The overall effect of such errors on the whole body of pupils who take a test will depend on how many boundaries there are and how these are spaced out. If the final mark is very close to a grade boundary a small shift in the examiners' judgment about this boundary might change a grade from (say) a C to a B for the same performance. For an examination which is for pass or fail, this factor will only give the wrong result for pupils close to the one borderline, whereas one with seven grades and six boundaries will involve more errors, although each error may matter less than when there are fewer boundaries.

Variability of Pupils from Day to Day

Any one pupil might have been more or less able to 'do justice to himself' on one day rather than another. This source seems to have received less attention than the others. To test its effect, one could set a group of pupils two 'parallel forms' of test, using the same types of questions and covering the same learning aims, on two occasions only a short time apart, and compare the two sets of results. One such experiment showed that half of those who failed one paper passed the other, and vice versa (Black, 1963, pp. 202–3). However, hardly any experiments of this type are reported in the literature.

Variability of Pupils from Question to Question

Any particular pupil might have done better in a test with a different set of questions — say those that will come up on next year's paper. This source receives a great deal of attention, and the problems which it raises are quite complex. There is a very large number of tasks that can be constructed to assess a pupil's attainment in any given area of learning. Even if the range is restricted to written responses, the particular topics and skills addressed in a question, the types of question used, the context in which the question is set, the way it is expressed can all be varied. There is ample evidence that all such variations can lead to significant variations in a pupil's response. Two questions which seem to the expert to be asking the same thing in different ways might well be seen by the pupil as completely different questions. One way to reduce the effect of such variations is to ask a large number of questions of different types and styles, but time and cost both limit the extent to which this can be done. The discussion here will be taken further in the section on Domain Referencing in Chapter 5.

Any practicable examination can sample only a limited number of the possibilities, and it is then important to be able to estimate how inaccurate the result might be because of this limitation. One way of doing this is to analyse the internal consistency of pupils' responses. If pupils each respond with about the same level of success to different questions, and if these questions are a fair sample of the possible range of relevant questions, then one can be confident that their overall score indicates accurately what these pupils might have attained over the full range of possibilities. A simple way to explore this is to divide any test paper into two halves and check the agreement between the marks for the separate halves. More complex techniques are equivalent to doing this, but they go further by averaging over the result of making the split into two halves in every possible way. A commonly used index of reliability for use with multiple choice tests is known as KR-20 (Kuder-Richardson); for tests where each question can earn a range of different marks, the index used is known as Cronbach-alpha. For both of these, the maximum ideal value is 1.0, and a value of around 0.85 to 0.95 is regarded as satisfactory. These indices are statistical indicators, in that they may be used to estimate the probability that any given mark might be in error by given amounts (Salvia and Ysseldyke, 1991, p. 132).

Such indices are often referred to as the reliability of a test — but such a claim must be treated with caution for three reasons, as follows:

- It is possible to select test questions so that a high value is obtained simply by making all the questions very similar. That could have two unfortunate consequences. One is that pupils might vary in the quality of answers to questions illustrated with (say) pictures compared with questions asked only with prose — some might be better at the one type, some at the other. Cutting out all questions with pictures will then increase these reliability indices, but in fact the test is now biased in favour of those who do better with prose. There would also be implications for the validity of the test — as discussed later in this chapter.

- The reliability will in fact vary across the score range. For example, the two pupils with scores of 90 per cent and 94 per cent respectively will have most of the questions correct and the difference between them can only depend on a very few questions. The reliability of very high or very low scores will not be the same as that for scores in the middle of the score range. For similar reasons, a test may discriminate well with a group of pupils having a wide range of attainment, but be far less reliable when used with a more narrowly selected group (Salvia and Ysseldyke, 1991, Chapter 7).
- All of the other sources of error, from marking, grading, and pupils' variability, are not reflected at all in these indices, so they are bound to give an optimistic picture of reliability.

The Reliability of a Test Result

All of these features represent threats to reliability. In most assessment systems, serious attempts are made to minimize their possible effects, but some are hard to deal with and it is inevitable that there will be a degree of error in any result. It is a quite formidable task to establish the reliability of any set of test scores. A review of research results over the past fifty years can show that the problems are potentially serious, and that they ought to be researched anew when new examination systems and procedures are introduced (Satterly, 1994, pp. 61–64). This need is widely neglected. It must be stressed however that the effects on pupils' results can be quite large. Even with a reliability coefficient that is high enough to be commonly regarded as acceptable (say 0.85 to 0.9), the errors in pupils' scores that are implied may mean that a significant proportion are given the wrong grade. The proportion so affected will clearly be greater the larger the number of grade boundaries involved (Wood, 1991, p. 135). A thorough exploration of reliability requires a technique which can allow for the simultaneous effects of different sources of error — this approach goes under the general title of generalizability theory (Shavelson and Webb, 1991).

An exploration of the effects of limited reliability for the UK Key Stage 3 National Tests (taken at age 14) showed that, using the index which was a measure only of the internal consistency factor, about 30 per cent of pupils would be placed in the wrong level — there is no way of knowing how much worse this figure might be if all of the factors could be taken into account (Wiliam, 1995).

All of the above discussion relates to the reliability of scores for individual pupils, and is therefore relevant to the formative and summative/certification purposes of assessments and tests. The issues change if the same test is applied to a group of pupils in order to obtain a general measure of the attainment of the group as a whole. In particular, errors due to the variability of an individual from day to day may be far less serious because the results are an average over many pupils. For errors due to the sensitivity of any one pupil's performance to the precise topic or format of a question will also tend to average out, although there may still be a systematic bias if the group as a whole had not covered certain topics or had not encountered certain types of question presentation. Such effects could be the features which the assessment was designed to reveal: they could only be regarded as errors if the test results were to be interpreted as a measure of the general potential or 'ability' of the pupils in the domain of the test.

Reliability issues will be different again if accountability measures are made by using only samples of pupils and giving different sets of questions or exercises to different sub-samples, the technique of matrix light sampling already referred to in Chapter 3. Provided that each sub-sample of pupils is large enough and representative, such a strategy will improve reliability by reducing the effect of variability across questions through the use of far larger numbers of questions (Johnson, 1988).

Validity

Many Varieties of Validity

A test composed of fifty multiple choice questions, all testing memory of the content of topics in a science curriculum, would raise no problems about reliability of marking and might give high reliability indices because its items were all rather similar. However, it could well be unsatisfactory. In part, this would be because it might not reflect the learning aims of the study of the pupils who were being tested. More importantly, the results would not give a fair indication of the capacity of the pupils to succeed in any future study of science: such future study would almost certainly involve a far broader set of aims than can be reflected by problems framed in an atomized form with pre-set responses set out for selection.

Such issues are examples of the general problem of validity. Many different aspects of validity have been explored and given their own special labels. A starting point might be to consider whether a test will measure what those who prepared it intended to measure. If, for example, there is some agreed aim of assessing competence in the subject, then experts might look at a test and consider whether in their judgment the questions would call for those performances which characterized that competence — this would be face validity. If the intention is to test that a given syllabus has been learnt, then examiners might check whether the questions matched the contents and learning aims of a syllabus, sampling the areas fairly and not going beyond its boundaries — this would be **content validity**. A more rigorous requirement would be that both the content covered and the cognitive or skill level of the test exercises should conform to a set of syllabus criteria. For these aspects, validity might be checked by expert judgment.

More difficult problems arise if the inferences drawn from the responses to a set of questions are more indirect. A notorious example is the construction and interpretation of intelligence tests: here, the sum of responses to a specific set of questions is said to measure something which is called 'intelligence', and predictions and actions affecting a pupil's future are then made on the basis of this measure. It is clearly necessary both to clarify conceptually the meaning of 'intelligence' and to explore, empirically or by expert judgment, whether a given set of questions do indeed require and evoke this as a common feature in the pupil's responses — such exploration might even call in question whether the abstract notion of intelligence represents a single coherent dimension of learning (Gardner, 1992). The focus here would be described as **construct validity**. Other examples would be tests of verbal reasoning, of numeracy, of creativity, and of spatial awareness. A great deal of effort is expended in the field of psychological testing in establishing the construct validity of psychological tests (Wood, 1991, pp. 150–5). The same issue will arise with tests more closely related to a teaching programme — examples here might be tests which claim to give a measure of historical understanding or of problem-solving in mathematics.

Checking on construct validity can be a complex matter. If a set of questions is said to bear on the same well-defined construct then there ought to be high correlation between the responses to them — here this aspect of reliability becomes a necessary condition to ensure validity. A tighter check would be to use, in the same test, a range of questions designed to address different constructs and to check that the inter-correlations between those which are claimed to measure the same construct are higher than between those for different constructs. A complementary approach would be to check that different types of question designed to assess the same construct show higher correlation than that between assessments of different constructs using the same types of question.

Consequential Validity

Many other varieties of validity — for example, curricular, instructional, concurrent, convergent, predictive, criterion — can be found in the literature, and most of these are clearly interdependent. However, it must be emphasized that an assessment instrument does not possess a validity in isolation — the validity depends on the way in which the result is to be interpreted. Some would argue that this point can justify an attempt to subsume the several varieties within a unified general approach. This focuses on the ways in which test results might be interpreted and is expressed in the following explanation by Messick.

> Validity is an integrated evaluative judgement of the degree to which empirical evidence and theoretical rationales support the *adequacy* and *appropriateness* of *inferences* and *actions* based on test scores or other modes of assessment. (Messick, 1989, p. 13; emphases as in the original)

The emphasis here is that the validity is a summary of the meanings behind a test score in terms of which it can be interpreted. Thus, a test is said to be valid if the inferences drawn from its results can be said to be justified in relation to these meanings. In this approach, judgment about the validity of a test can only be made in relation to the purposes it is meant to serve and the uses to which the results should be put. Indeed, one objection to this approach is that in many situations, test designers cannot control the interpretations which people might place on the results and so cannot be responsible for them.

The inferences that might be drawn from a test result fall into two main categories. One type of inference might look forward to the future performance of a student in new learning programmes or in remedial work on the previous programme. The other might look back at the previous learning programme and so lead to changes to improve test results for future students.

The forward inference is referred to as **predictive validity**. One way to check on this aspect of validity seems relatively straightforward — the inferences made can be explored in relation to the future achievements of those affected by them. Thus, one might look for correlation between results of tests used to select for university entrance and the degree performance of those admitted. It must be emphasized that the basis for understanding the prediction is the interpretation of the test scores, rather than a blind pursuit of empirical correlations. The need for caution is illustrated by the common result that the correlation between A-level and degree results is low (say 0.5 or less). The usual inference drawn from this is that A-level results are not useful for selecting for entry to degree courses. This inference is quite unjustified for the following reasons:

- It would be easy if all those who took a test were admitted to degree study irrespective of their results, but this does not happen. Only those who attain above a certain level are available for the study, so the sample has only a narrow range of marks at the upper end of the score distribution of the selection test. Whilst the correlation over the full range of scores might have been quite high, because over the full range the effects of unreliability were comparatively small, the correlation for the attenuated range of those admitted might be low because the same unreliability effects are now comparatively large (Guilford and Fruchter, 1973, p. 315).
- Neither of the two sets of scores that are being correlated is perfectly reliable. Given that both have limited reliability, it might

be possible to estimate the maximum correlation that might be obtained for the observed scores if the two scores were in fact perfectly correlated and the correlation only lowered by errors of unreliability — this would give an upper limit of the correlation that might be obtained. However, the reliability of the two components is usually unknown.

- Even given the best possible predictor, a high index of correlation should not be expected. Higher level study calls on and develops new capability in students and they themselves will change in many ways over the years of degree study — indeed, a perfect correlation might call in question whether the degree course had changed its students in any important ways.

Such checks become more complicated where the validity of more abstract constructs is involved. For example, if an intelligence test is meant to be an indicator of general ability to succeed with cognitive tasks over a wide range, then correlations might have to be sought with many indicators of future performance, separately or in combination.

Any discussion of the backward inference raises broad questions about validity in relation to the effects of assessment on learning. This issue is taken up in the next main section.

Validity and Learning

Teaching to the Test

There is extensive evidence that 'high-stakes' testing constrains both teachers and pupils to align their learning to meeting the demands of tests. For example, in England and Wales the practices of primary teachers in teaching mathematics are being altered as it becomes important for their schools that their pupils perform well in the national assessments at age 11 (Gipps *et al.*, 1995) and science teachers have expressed their opinion that their teaching has narrowed in response to the pressures of the tests at age 14 (ASE, 1992). This alignment can be more close than is often realized. Further examples to justify this statement are discussed in the section of Chapter 5 on norm referencing.

Thus external tests can be powerful influences on teaching and learning. Whether these are evaluated as beneficial or malign will depend on the qualities of the test and the assumptions about learning adopted by the evaluator. The principle underlying this nexus between testing and learning can be stated quite clearly:

Assessments must be so designed that when you do the natural thing — that is, prepare the students to perform well — they will exercise the kinds of abilities and develop the kinds of skills that are the real goals of educational reform. (Resnick and Resnick, 1992, p. 59)

Atomized Learning and Atomized Tests

It is important to look carefully at the assumptions about learning that may underlie the construction of any test. If these do not reflect the assumptions that inform the prior learning of those tested, or if the assumptions are ill-judged in relation to potential for future learning, then the test will be invalid. Of course, the first of these two disjunctions may be removed if the test is high-stakes — teachers will teach to the test and the prior learning of those tested will be forced to work to the assumptions of the testers. The following extracts, taken from two articles in Gifford and O'Connor illustrate and develop an argument about the links between testing methods and beliefs about learning.

The most important contribution . . . is the insight that all learning involves thinking. It is incorrect to believe, according to old learning theory, that the basics can be taught by rote followed by thinking and reasoning. As documented by the Resnicks, even comprehension of simple texts requires a process of inferring and thinking about what the text means. Children who are drilled in number facts, algorithms, decoding skills or vocabulary lists without developing a basic conceptual model or seeing the meaning of what they are doing have a very difficult time retaining information (because all the bits are disconnected) and are unable to apply what they have memorised (because it makes no sense).

. . . 'measurement-driven instruction' will lead reform in the wrong direction if tests embody incomplete or low-level learning goals.

Various efforts to reform assessment use terms such as 'authentic,' 'direct' and 'performance' assessment to convey the idea that assessments must capture real learning activities if they are to avoid distorting instruction. (Shepard, 1992, pp. 303–4; 325)

The article by Resnick and Resnick (1992), to which Shepard refers, develops a critique of the multiple choice or very short answer tests which were until recently almost the only form of testing in USA schools:

Children who practice reading mainly in the form in which it appears in the tests — and there is good evidence that this is what happens in many classrooms — would have little exposure to the demands and reasoning possibilities of the thinking curriculum.

Students who practised mathematics in the form found in the standardized tests would never be exposed to the kind of mathematical thinking sought by all who are concerned with reforming mathematical education, ranging from people involved with practical instruction to those interested in more academic forms of mathematical activity. (pp. 46–7)

The authors conclude that:

If widely adopted as part of the public accountability assessment system, performance assessments (including portfolio assessments) could not only remove current pressures for teaching isolated collections of facts and skills but also provide a positive stimulus for introducing more extended thinking and reasoning activities in the curriculum. (op. cit., p. 68)

These extracts explore the relationship of testing to a particular approach to learning, which emphasizes the learning by rote, of small pieces of knowledge — without the understanding which interrelates them, and of fixed rules and procedures. Where this is done, these rules and procedures will be grasped only as tactics without the strategic overview needed to give them significance and to guide their application. The tests that are appropriate to this atomized approach to learning will consist of many short items and it will be easy, both to select from these and to have enough of them to achieve high internal consistency within a test, and to ensure reliability in the marking. Thus there is a symbiosis — some would say a conspiracy — between tests which can achieve high reliability at low cost, and teaching and learning methods which have long been accepted as adequate and which have a simplistic appeal. The inadequacy of the model of learning inevitably implies a lack of validity in the tests.

Problems of Improved Assessment

However, to follow the Resnick's goal of establishing tests which reflect and so encourage 'extended thinking and reasoning activities in the curriculum' raises a host of difficulties. Extended tasks take time. Insofar as they should be open to different possible interpretations and different types of valid response, it will be more difficult to ensure marking procedures which are consistent across many different types of response and which reflect performance against common, albeit general, criteria. Finally, for a given cost, it may only be possible to replace an external test of (say) 50 multiple choice items by a test comprising one or two extended tasks. Here again, reliability may be compromised since any one pupil's performance may vary widely from one particular task context to another (Shavelson *et al.*, 1993; discussed further in Chapter 6).

Christie explains a different type of difficulty which arises in the assessment of reading. A pupil's performance on a reading task will depend both on the context of the task and on her reading skills. It follows that the notion of a general reading skill, divorced from any particular context, is meaningless and any attempt to measure it is futile. As Christie (1995) puts it:

> A single dimension, the testing objective of the 1920s, is disastrous from the pedagogical point of view. How can teachers respond to such a score? It is a single number and all the teacher can endeavour to do is to make it larger. In these circumstances teaching to the test is the only sensible strategy but, as Goodhart's law demonstrates in economics, attempts to manipulate a predictive variable, rather than to manipulate the performance that the variable predicts, immediately destroy the set of relationships which lent the variable predictive validity in the first place. The mini-economy of our classrooms echoes our nation's economic plight. Ritualistic behaviour is rife. (p. 112)

What this means in practice is that if the reader, for example, uses a particular skill selectively according to context, then one cannot report on attainment in a 'skill' dimension and report separately on attainment in a 'context' dimension. Christie's point here is made in the context of an argument for the essentially multi-dimensional nature of reading. A construct driven assessment is driven to be uni-dimensional and a test theory driven by such an approach is bound to fail. The skill can only be tested in authentic tasks — a decontextualized surrogate skill task gives no useful information, because nothing can be inferred from it about use of the skill in any particular context.

Links Between Reliability and Validity

The confidence that an assessment result can command will clearly depend on both the reliability and the validity. A test giving scores which are reproducible over a wide variety of conditions (i.e. a reliable test) would nevertheless be of no value if the attainment that it measures is irrelevant to (say) the learning being explored, or if that attainment is too narrow an aspect of the whole to be of any significance (i.e. an invalid test). A set of test items which clearly reflect the aims of a course and can be seen to evoke the type of performance that the course aimed to promote (i.e. a valid test) is of little value if it turns out that examiners cannot agree on how to mark the outcomes, or if a different set of apparently comparable items would produce very different scores with the same pupils on a different occasion (i.e. an unreliable test). If it turned out that there was no correlation between a test score and the future attainment that it was designed to predict, then it could be that either or both of the reliability and the validity of the test were defective.

The two aspects are not entirely independent. For example, as explained above, one check on construct validity would be the inter-correlation between relevant test items. If this inter-correlation were low neither criterion is satisfied, whereas if it were high, the test would satisfy one criterion for reliability; it could also be a valid measure of the intended construct, although it is always possible that it is actually measuring something else. For example, a test designed to measure comprehension using a set of different and varied questions about a given prose passage might turn out to be testing familiarity with the subject content of the passage rather than the ability to understand unseen prose passages in general. Similarly, as also pointed out above, for predictive validity an adequate reliability is a necessary, but not a sufficient condition.

Whether or not reliability is an essential prior condition for validity will depend on the circumstances and purposes of an assessment. Two different cases will illustrate this point, as follows:

- For any test or assessment where decisions are taken which cannot easily be changed, as in examinations for public certificates, reliability will be an essential prior condition for validity. However, there may be a high price to pay, because the testing might have to take a long time and there would have to be careful checks on the marking and grading to ensure the reliability required. Given limited resources, the two ideals of validity and reliability may often be in conflict. Narrowing the range of the testing aims can make it possible to enhance reliability at the expense of validity, whilst broadening the range might do the reverse.

- Such conditions would not apply in the same way to classroom assessment by a teacher. In classroom use, an action taken on the basis of a result can easily be changed if it turns out that the result is misleading so that the action is inappropriate. In these circumstances, a teacher may infer that a pupil has grasped an idea on the basis of achievement on one piece of work and may not wish to spend the time needed in order to ensure high reliability — by taking an average of a pupil's performance over several tasks — before moving the pupil on to the next piece of work. However, this decision that the pupil should move on would be quite unjustified if the achievement result were invalid, for then it would bear no relation to what the pupil might need as a basis for moving on to the next piece of work. (Wiliam and Black, 1996)

Bias

Many Sources of Bias: Differential Item Functioning

In the original development of Binet's intelligence test, it was found at one stage that the mean score for girls was higher than that for boys. Items for which the excess of the girls scores over the boys scores was particularly large were sought out and enough of them were removed to make the means for the two groups the same. There is no absolute or objective way of determining whether or not this was a reasonable procedure. It was notable however that other possible differences between other sub-groups were not so analysed at the time.

There are many ways in which questions might be unfair in their impact between different pupils. Six of the most common possibilities may be explained as follows:

- An assessment which used questions set in the context of mechanical toys would almost certainly lead to higher scores for boys than for girls, whereas one set using examples and situations from dolls or kitchen work would favour girls.
- Whilst a test may have an explicit bias if gender stereotyping is built in to the question, it may have a less obvious bias: for example, essay questions will favour boys if they are on impersonal topics, and will favour girls if they relate to human and personal implications.
- In general, girls do not perform as well as boys on multiple-choice items, but do better on essay-type questions. A possible reason for this is that girls are less likely than boys to guess when they do not know the answer.
- The course-work components at 16-plus in the GCSE examinations may be one of the factors responsible for the enhanced performances of girls compared with boys — thought to be because girls are more disadvantaged by the anxieties attendant on a formal-timed test.
- A question may only be intelligible within certain cultural and social assumptions — for example, a question about old people living on their own describes a situation which is fairly normal in a western white culture, but which is abnormal in other cultures and would lead some pupils to look for unusual reasons why the old person had been excluded from the family.
- Similarly, a test set using middle class language or conventions would favour children of one social class, or with a particular home language background, against another.

There is a whole class therefore of 'between groups' differences, of which the gender differences are one example, which arise from the context in which any assessment exercise is based. Such effects have been widely researched. They are quite predictable, so that it might not be difficult to avoid at least the most common of them. However, there are subtle difficulties. For example, in England there are differences in the mean IQ scores between black and white children and between children with families in different economic circumstances. However, whether or not these differences are due to test bias or reflect real differences with other origins — for example in denial of educational opportunities — is not easy to determine (Wood, 1991, Chapter 14, pp. 178–9; Macintosh, 1986).

There is almost endless scope for analyses of differences in test scores between different groups who attempt it — and in cases where a difference is found there may then be a dilemma as to whether the difference is objective or an artefact of the items — i.e. the test is biased. Bias in a test arises when people equally good at the attainment being tested obtain different scores — the technical phrase 'differential-item functioning' expresses this principle.

Differential item-functioning has to be explored in two ways. One is to scrutinize questions for any well-known sources of bias. Given that this can never be enough, the other approach is to try out the questions on samples of pupils representing different genders and different ethnic and social groups, to look for variations between the responses from the different groups, and then to wrestle with the dilemmas of interpreting these differences and of redressing them, or not, in the light of the purpose of the assessment. The analyses involved here can raise difficult technical issues (Wood, 1991, pp. 176–7).

Finally, there may be bias at the individual, rather than group, level which such procedures cannot reveal. Typical differences between the means of scores for boys and girls on a test are usually very small compared with the spread of the scores for both groups. Indeed, one might regard (say) revealed gender effects simply as crude average signs of biases which run across genders — for example, some boys may be better at essay type questions than at multiple choice and are therefore disadvantaged if essay questions are not used. Averaging over many different types of question may help reduce unfairness, but may be misleading. One pupil may show her true strength in one particular test mode, another in a different way. The average over many ways may be a mediocre score for both which underrates their competence.

Taking Action

It is possible to adjust the construction of assessment methods to deal with many of the effects of bias and discrimination which might have caused differences in the scores of different groups — although whether or not action is taken may depend on the purpose and the context of testing. For example, by adjusting the mix between multiple-choice and essay questions, it would be possible to ensure that girls have the same group average as boys. To do this would be to work for equality of outcomes. Such processes of adjustment may be difficult to justify, except perhaps in terms of some wider motives of social engineering. Indeed, they would be counter-productive if the purpose of the testing was to reveal effects of discriminatory practice in education.

On the other hand, if a particular minority were to be disadvantaged by being denied opportunity to learn one aspect (say) of a syllabus, then for some predictive purposes it would be important that the test be confined to those areas of knowledge and skill which the students have had an opportunity to learn. The principle of equity being illustrated here is that the test should be adjusted to ensure equality of access. A useful suggestion by Goldstein, is to distinguish 'group difference', which is an empirical fact, from 'bias', which is a judgment about the relevance or irrelevance of that difference to the attribute being assessed (Goldstein, 1996, p. 89). In many cases, such a judgment cannot be made on technical grounds alone, it has to be based on the social values and political purposes entailed in the assessment.

Little is known about bias effects in assessment practices within schools. All of the features mentioned above are potential sources of bias in both formative and summative assessments by teachers. Where teachers know their pupils well, they might be able to detect and act upon individual or group differences, by adapting the tasks or by making allowances in interpreting results. However, matters could be worse if favouritism towards, or stereotyping of, pupils by their teachers leads to differential expectations and so to bias in assessing the attainments of different pupils. This issue is discussed further in Chapter 7.

Equity in Assessment and the Law

Test procedures are always likely to come under scrutiny by agencies responsible for ensuring civil rights (the US phrase) or equal opportunities (the UK phrase), and also in the courts. Agencies who have the duty of identifying and removing any mechanisms of unfair discrimination ought to look at any assessment procedure which can affect careers and employment. Thus, for example, tests used to select applicants for posts have been examined in court rooms where educational systems and employers have been sued for unfair practices. In a classic case in the US (*Larry P. vs. Riles*) the practice of the state of California in using standardized tests to place children in special classes designed for the 'educable mentally retarded' was prohibited. There were disproportionate numbers of black children in such classes, but the state argued that the use of the IQ tests was valid because there were good correlations between their results and subsequent school grades and scores on achievement tests. The judge's ruling made a significant distinction:

> If tests can predict that a person is going to be a poor employee, the employer can legitimately deny that person a job, but if tests suggest that a young child is probably going to be a poor student, the school cannot on that basis deny the child the opportunity to improve and develop the academic skills necessary to success in our society. (quoted in Linn, 1989, p. 7)

A Complex Problem

It should by now be clear that the study of bias, and the pursuit of equity, are complex ventures. In summarizing their detailed study of equity in assessment, Gipps and Murphy (1994) conclude:

> By now it should be clear that there is no such thing as a fair test, nor could there be: the situation is too complex and the notion simplistic. However, by paying attention to what we know about factors in assessment and their administration and scoring, we can begin to work towards tests that are more fair to all groups likely to be taking them, and this is particularly important for assessment used for summative and accountability purposes. (p. 273)

What may be in question is whether there is adequate research information about the threats to equity across all the different backgrounds, whether of gender, or ethnicity, or social background, or cognitive preference and learning style, or temperament, to provide a basis for working towards tests that may be as fair as possible to all.

Conclusion

The key concept in this chapter is that of validity. It is a difficult concept theoretically, and its over-riding importance in assessment practice is honoured more in the breach than in the observance. In general, partly because it is difficult to research, the study of validity has been much neglected. For example, Wood (1991), writing in a study commissioned by an examination board, concluded as follows:

> The examining boards have been lucky not to have been engaged in a validity argument. Unlike reliability, validity does not lend itself to sensational reporting. Nevertheless, the extent of the boards' neglect of validity is plain to see once attention is focused. . . . The boards know so little about what they are assessing. (p. 151)

However, good quality assessment is inevitably the child of a union between reliability and validity. The offspring has to be nurtured with careful attention to the service of good learning, and of promotion of social justice through vigilance in matters of bias.

Most of the discussion has focused mainly on external tests designed for summative and for accountability purposes. This is not because the issues are less important for formative assessment, but because they have not been studied to anything like the same extent for the classroom context, where they will raise different, but equally difficult, problems. Reliability will have to be judged by quite different criteria and methods, whilst the link between valid test measures and the nature of the learning scheme for students is even more intimate if we look at the level of day to day classroom assessments. This was emphasized in Chapter 3, and the point bears repetition in the present context, calling again on the statement by Linn (1989):

> ... the design of tests useful for the instructional decisions made in the classroom requires an integration of testing and instruction. It also requires a clear conception of the curriculum, the goals, and the process of instruction. And it requires a theory of instruction and learning and a much better understanding of the cognitive processes of learners. (p. 5)

Validity in relation to effective models of learning must be the overriding priority for formative classroom assessment, but, as the above extract makes clear, it is a formidable task.

Summary

- Confidence in assessments depends on the criteria of reliability, validity and absence of bias.
- Reliability depends on whether the results are reproducible with different markers, grading procedures, test occasions, and different sets of questions.
- Reliability is in principle easy to check, but in practice the effects of only some of the sources are examined and comprehensive estimates of reliability are rarely available.
- Validity is a complex concept, best summarized as consequential validity, which focuses on whether the inferences and actions based on a test result can be justified.
- Validity is very difficult to check and is widely neglected. There is need to examine both the forward aspect — in relation to predictions, and the backward aspect — in relation to effects of testing on learning.
- The relative importance of reliability and validity depends on the purposes of an assessment; they can be in competition in that one can often be enhanced only at the expense of the other.

- The close interaction between assessment practices and learning practices means that the validity of assessments is linked to models of learning used in pedagogy.
- There are many sources of bias in assessment; some are hard to detect, and even when they are understood, the issues of whether or not to correct for them raise deeper questions about social values in relation to the assessment purposes.
- The serious responsibilities of those making assessment judgments are reflected in legal liabilities, particularly in relation to the rights of groups who may be disadvantaged by test bias.
- For all of the issues summarized above, there has been extensive research and writing in relation to the summative practices and very little in relation to the formative.

Bibliography

CROCKER, L. and ALGINA, J. (1986) *An Introduction to Classical and Modern Test Theory*, New York: Holt, Rinehart and Winston. This gives a detailed and sophisticated treatment both of reliability in Chapters 6 to 9 (including an introduction to generalizability theory in Chapter 8), and of validity in Chapters 10 to 13, with further detail on bias in Chapter 16.

GIFFORD, B.R. and O'CONNOR, M.C. (1992) *Changing Assessments: Alternative Views of Aptitude, Achievement and Instruction.* Boston and Dordrecht: Kluwer. This concentrates on the relationship between assessment practices and learning theory.

GIPPS, C.V. (1994) *Beyond Testing: Towards a Theory of Educational Assessment*, London: Falmer. Chapter 4 for validity and reliability and Chapter 8 on ethics and equity.

GIPPS, C. and MURPHY, P. (1994) *A Fair Test? Assessment, Achievement and Equity*, Buckingham: Open University Press. A full discussion of the issues pertaining to bias, with a comprehensive review of the literature.

GIPPS, C. and STOBART, G. (1993) *Assessment. A Teachers' Guide to the Issues*, London: Hodder and Stoughton. Chapter 2 for validity and Chapter 5 for equal opportunities and bias.

LINN, R.L. (ed.) (1989) *Educational Measurement (3rd. edn.)*, New York and London: Macmillan and American Council on Education. A standard professional reference work; Chapter 2 on Validity by Messick is a seminal article, Chapter 3 on reliability and Chapter 5 on bias in test use also give thorough reviews.

SALVIA, J. and YSSELDYKE, J.E. (1991) *Assessment*, Boston: Houghton Mifflin. Chapters 7 on reliability and 8 on validity give helpful explanations of the statistical principles related to these two concept areas; Chapter 3 on legal and ethical considerations is also a good summary of issues in law and practice in the USA.

WAINER, H. and BRAUN, H.I. (eds) (1988) *Test Validity*, Hillsdale NJ: Lawrence Erlbaum. A wide ranging treatment of many different aspects of validity, in fourteen chapters contributed by many of the leading US scholars in the field.

WITTROCK, M.C. and BAKER, E.L. (eds) (1991) *Testing and Cognition*. Englewood Cliffs, NJ: Prentice Hall. A collection of nine articles, seven covering general issues in the psychology of learning in relation to assessment principles, and two focused on practical implications for testing, in mathematics and in history respectively.

WOOD, R. (1991) *Assessment and Testing*, Cambridge: Cambridge University Press. See Chapter 11 on reliability, 12 on validity and 14 on bias.

References

ASE (1992) 'Key Stage 3 Monitoring Group: Report on the monitoring of Key Stage 3', *Education in Science*, November, pp. 18–19.

BLACK, P.J. (1963) 'Examinations and the teaching of science', *Bulletin of the Institute of Physics and the Physical Society*, pp. 202–3.

CHRISTIE, T. (1995) 'Defining the reading domain', in OWEN, P. and PUMFREY, P. (eds) *Children Learning to Read: International Concerns Vol 2. Curriculum and Assessment Issues: Messages for Teachers*, London: Falmer Press, pp. 107–20.

GARDNER, H. (1992) 'Assessment in context: The alternative to standardized testing', in GIFFORD, B.R. and O'CONNOR, M.C. (eds) *Changing Assessments: Alternative Views of Aptitude, Achievement and Instruction*, Boston and Dordrecht: Kluwer, pp. 77–117.

GIPPS, C.V. (1994) *Beyond Testing: Towards a Theory of Educational Assessment*, London: Falmer Press.

GIPPS, C., BROWN, M., McCALLUM, B. and McALISTER, S. (1995) *Intuition or Evidence? Teachers and National Assessment of 7-year-olds*, Buckingham: Open University Press.

GIPPS, C. and MURPHY, P. (1994) *A Fair Test? Assessment, Achievement and Equity*, Buckingham: Open University Press.

GOLDSTEIN, H. (1996) 'Group differences and bias in assessment', in GOLDSTEIN, H. and LEWIS, T. (eds) *Assessment: Problems, Developments and Statistical Issues*, Chichester and New York: John Wiley, pp. 85–93.

GUILDFORD, J.P. and FRUCHTER, B. (1973) *Fundamental Statistics in Psychology and Education*, (5th edn.) New York: McGraw Hill, p. 315.

JOHNSON, S. (1988) *National Assessment: The APU Science Approach*, London: HMSO.

LINN, R.L. (1989) 'Current perspectives and future directions', in LINN, R.L. (ed.) *Educational Measurement*, 3rd edition, New York and London: Macmillan and American Council on Education, pp. 1–10.

MACINTOSH, N.J. (1986) 'The biology of intelligence', *British Journal of Psychology*, 77, pp. 1–18.

MESSICK, S. (1989) 'Validity', in LINN, R.L. (ed.) *Educational Measurement*, (3rd edn.) New York and London: Macmillan and American Council on Education.

RESNICK, L.R. and RESNICK, D.P. (1992) 'Assessing the thinking curriculum: New tools for educational reform', in GIFFORD, B.R. and O'CONNOR, M.C. (eds) *Changing Assessments: Alternative Views of Aptitude, Achievement and Instruction*, Boston and Dordrecht: Kluwer, pp. 37–75.

SALVIA, J. and YSSELDYKE, J.E. (1991) *Assessment*, Boston: Houghton Mifflin.

SATTERLY, D. (1994) 'Quality in external assessment', in HARLEN, W. (ed.) *Enhancing Quality in Assessment,* London: Paul Chapman, pp. 53–70.

SHAVELSON, R.J., BAXTER, G.P. and GAO, X. (1993) 'Sampling variability of perform-ance assessments', *Journal of Educational Measurement,* **30**, 3, pp. 215–32.

SHAVELSON, R.J. and WEBB, N.M. (1991) *Generalizability Theory: A Primer,* London: Sage (n.b. This book assumes an understanding of analysis of variance).

SHEPARD, L.A. (1992) 'Commentary: What policy makers who mandate tests should know about the new psychology of intellectual ability and learning', in GIFFORD, B.R. and O'CONNOR, M.C. (eds) *Changing Assessments: Alternative Views of Aptitude, Achievement and Instruction,* Boston and Dordrecht: Kluwer, pp. 301–28.

UNIVERSITY OF CAMBRIDGE LOCAL EXAMINATIONS SYNDICATE (1976) *School Examina-tions and their Function,* Cambridge: UCLES.

WILIAM, D. (1995) 'It'll all end in tiers', *British Journal of Curriculum and Assess-ment,* **5**, 3, pp. 21–4.

WILIAM, D. and BLACK, P.J. (1996) 'Meanings and consequences: A basis for distin-guishing formative and summative functions of assessment', *British Educational Research Journal,* **22**, 5, pp. 537–48.

WOOD, R. (1991) *Assessment and Testing,* Cambridge: Cambridge University Press. See Chapter 11 on reliability, 12 on validity and 14 on bias.

Chapter 5

What to Test — Norms, Criteria and Domains

Introduction

The decisions about what to test, the interpretation of test results and the purposes for which a test is being used are all inter-linked issues. This chapter focuses on one of the key features which links these issues. Put very simply, the issue bears upon the differences between the following statements about a pupil, judging that he or she:

- is the fourth in the class in arithmetic;
- can add pairs of two digit numbers;
- has achieved basic competence in arithmetic;
- has reached level 4 in arithmetic.

Each of these can be a useful statement for some particular purpose. Each carries a different meaning. Each has to be based on evidence, or on interpretation of evidence, in a different way. The first four sections of this chapter will deal in succession with these four types of statement, discussing in sequence norm referencing, criterion referencing, domain referencing and progression in learning. In so doing they will have to explore the relationship of these features to issues of learning and pedagogy. The implications of the issues for the assignments of grades and for debates about standards will then be examined. A final section will examine more generally the issues of interpretation in relation to purpose.

Norm Referencing

Terms, Meanings, Methods

Whether or not one is interested in knowing that a pupil is tenth in the class depends on one's assumptions and priorities in the business of learning. If the model is one of competition then the result is informative, but if on the other hand one wants to know how capable the pupil is in arithmetic or how much of what was taught he or she has mastered, the result is of little use. The difference here might be sharpened by one's underlying belief about human ability and attainment. The result might indicate that the pupil is well above average in ability — some might say that this is all that matters and the other questions are matters of local and transient detail.

A test result which is expressed in relation to the distribution of results amongst a group is said to be norm referenced. The IQ result given by an intelligence test is a common example. Such a test will have been administered to a large sample of the population, and the distribution of results will follow the normal bell-shaped curve. Any individual's result can then be expressed in relation to this distribution curve. For IQ tests all scores are usually scaled to give a mean value of 100. The spread of the scores is then adjusted so that the standard deviation is 15, which means that two-thirds of the population have scores within the range 115 and 85. It is then possible to find the relative significance of any other score — for example, for a score of 70 one can find out that 98.5 per cent of the population will have scored more than this and 1.5 per cent will have scored less. The norms used here are the mean and the spread for the population as a whole.

A common method for expressing scores on a norm based approach is to first calculate the deviation from the mean (so 70 is expressed as minus 30) and then give this deviation as a fraction of the standard deviation, so that, given a standard deviation of 15, a score of minus 30 is expressed as minus 2 standard deviations. This would be known as a Z-score. Other ways of expressing such scores — t-scores, stanines, CEEB scores — all involve some simple transformation of the raw score (Hanna, 1993, pp. 451–3).

Norm referenced tests are thus characterized by two concerns. One is about the sample used to establish these norms. The sample has to be large enough and has to be typical of the population to which reference is being made. Being in the top 10 per cent of class 3B might be the same as being in the top 10 per cent of the year group if class 3B is typical of the whole year group. One could not assert that the pupil was in the top 10 per cent for the whole country unless a far wider and carefully chosen sample had been used to 'normalize', i.e. calibrate the test. Where results are expressed in relation to a particular group, they should be described as 'cohort-referenced' to distinguish them from the more ambitious aim of reference to a whole age group across a country.

The second concern is about the selection of the items used. The purpose of the test is to discriminate, to spread out the population. Test items on which all succeeded would be of no value and would be removed during test development, even though the fact that everybody can succeed on a particular task might be useful information for other purposes. Similarly, items on which nobody can succeed will be removed.

Insofar as tests of this type yield distributions which follow the bell-shaped curve which would be expected from the assumptions of classical statistical theory, the results can be manipulated and analysed according to that theory. In consequence, norm-referenced tests can be subject to powerful methods of analysis, but in consequence also they tend to become the property of psychometric experts rather than of educators.

Can Norms Change?

As pointed out in Chapter 2, the growth in importance of IQ testing was fuelled in part by beliefs in the innate and genetically determined nature of human intelligence. Within such beliefs, the main purpose of testing is to sort out the population. Teaching and learning have little to do with the exercise if one believes that intelligence is not susceptible to improvement by instruction, and for some social purposes the test is more fair if high quality schooling does not confer an advantage in test performance.

There are problems raised by such assumptions even in the realm of intelligence testing and the associated realm of scholastic aptitude tests (for example, the USA SATs). However, the principles of norm-referenced testing have been carried over into far wider areas. In public examinations in the UK, such as the GCSE, the overall scores are used to allocate candidates to grades and attention is paid to the proportions of the entry so allocated. If those proportions change from one year to the next, public concern is aroused — or stirred up — about changes in the standards. Of course, the existence of changes shows that the examination is not strictly norm referenced: it is not clear whether those who raise public concern about the change would want them to have the same distribution each and every year — thus imposing the assumption that overall performance cannot change with time. Similarly, difficult problems arise when the distributions of scores, or grades derived from scores, are compared across subjects. If the populations entering are different between subjects, as is the case for A-levels in England, there is no *a priori* reason to expect comparability of outcomes. In the case of subjects taken by all, for example, English and mathematics in GCSE, the issue is a more difficult one. Such arguments highlight the key feature of norm-referenced results — they place the entry population in rank order, they tell you little about what that rank order means.

Standardized Tests and Lake Wobegon

A large number of tests is available, mainly through commercial test agencies, which are designed to help identify particular aspects of 'ability' or 'aptitude' and also to measure some basic features of learning achievement, as in tests of reading or numeracy (Levy and Goldstein 1984, Buros). Most of these tests are 'standardized'. This means that the publisher has tested them on an adequately large and representative sample, and then the user can tell how well a particular class, or school, or whole region, is performing in relation to a national average. Where the purpose of testing is to ensure the accountability of schools, this is an attractive feature.

However, there are here some serious traps for the unwary. Tests of this type are in use to survey either reading, or numeracy, or both, in thirty-five of the fifty states of the USA. There is controversy over whether they test what they are supposed to test — even, as in the case of reading, whether the attainment of interest can be tested at all by such methods (Gipps and Stobart, 1993, pp. 67–9). Even if this problem is overcome, there are others.

Surveys of the reported results have revealed that across different ages and in the two subjects almost all of these states show mean performances above the average, and that even at the finer grain level of school districts the majority are above average (Linn *et al.*, 1990). A similar absurdity is featured in one of Garrison Keiller's stories and so this phenomenon has been called, after his fictional location, the Lake Wobegon effect. Several reasons can be offered for this effect:

- The norms are based on data that are several years old and the schools' performance is improving with time.
- Norms are established by the voluntary participation of schools in trials and the sample so secured may be biased in some way — for example, more pupils may be excluded from 'real' tests than from trials.
- Schools who are under pressure to produce good test results will train their pupils to do well in the particular test that is used; insofar as the training is effective, it defeats the purpose of the tests — which is to yield results which are independent of the particular curriculum followed.

There is some evidence to support all three proposed explanations. In particular, it has been shown in several US districts that norm-based performance scores can fall by the equivalent of over half a school year's progress when one particular form of test is replaced by another. What usually happens subsequently is that the scores rise again over four to five years until the norm score on the new form is the same as it was on the old one before the change. In one district where this had happened, a sample of those whose performance had recovered after five years were also given the old test on which their predecessors had done equally well five years ago. This sample showed a far poorer performance on the old test, at a level similar to that of their predecessors on the new test when it had first been introduced (Linn, 1994).

The conclusion must be that results from standardized tests have to be treated with a great deal of caution. In particular, where they are used for 'high stakes' accountability, they can be self-defeating in that test-directed teaching can produce effects which are artefacts of the accountability regime itself rather than generalizable evidence of change in learning.

Criterion Referencing

Meaning

The example quoted in the Introduction: 'can add pairs of two digit numbers' is typical of a criterion-referenced result. The result gives explicit information about what has been learned. The test used would usually be composed to reflect the aims of the teaching, and the information gained could be used for formative purposes. The distinction between norm-referencing and criterion-referencing is not necessarily a distinction between tests as such. For example, the addition of scores over many questions in a standardized test may yield norm based information, whilst the success or failure of a pupil on a particular question might give criterion-information.

In general, however, there will be two main differences. The criterion emphasis will mean that questions are selected for their relevance to the teaching and learning programme, whereas for a standardized test this is unimportant — indeed if the assumption is that some innate property not directly related to teaching is to be measured, such questions might be rejected.

A second difference relates to the success of pupils in answering the questions. Imagine a test in which 80 per cent to 90 per cent of pupils could answer all of the questions. This might be useful, in confirming that a basic understanding had been established, so that the learning could move ahead to work on topics depending on that understanding, and also in identifying the small proportion of pupils who needed extra and immediate help to remove an obstacle to their progress. For normative purposes such a test would be useless, because it would not discriminate between the majority of the pupils. Items that are very easy or very hard would all be eliminated in the development of a normative test, in order that the test scores would spread out the performances.

Norms and Criteria — Two Perspectives

It is unhelpful to think of 'norm-referenced' and 'criterion-referenced' as phrases which describe two completely different types of test. Instead, norm and criterion should be seen as two different sets of properties possessed by every test and/or by the possible interpretations of its results. Thus a qualifying test for a competitor in an athletics event may well be that they can surpass two metres in a high jump — a very clear criterion. But this criterion has only been chosen in the light of normative data showing that there are enough athletes, and not too many, who can achieve this level. Similarly, the items for a standardized test of numeracy will be trialled and selected to yield the optimum statistical properties for the test, but they must nevertheless satisfy the criterion of being relevant to significant aspects of numeracy.

The balance between norm and criterion aspects will be related to the purposes of the testing and assessment. Formative assessment clearly requires criterion referencing, although, as for the high-jump case, the criteria have to be attainable by a significant proportion of the pupils concerned. For tests designed to serve accountability the position is less clear. Placing schools in rank order is a different priority from assessing whether or not they are following the national curriculum, let alone one of evaluating the appropriateness of that curriculum. The former requires the discriminating properties of a normative test, the latter requires the educationally relevant properties of criterion-referencing.

The summative purpose lies between these two. A collection of criterion-referenced scores might best serve the purpose — for a receiving school may be more interested in what a pupil can or cannot do than in where that pupil may be placed in some normal distribution of test scores. The same might be true of potential employers: however, such employers might judge that the talents that their enterprises needed were not directly related to specific aspects of school learning and might therefore look for the 'best' pupils on a norm basis, perhaps supplementing this information with IQ or other aptitude tests of their own.

Broad or Narrow Criteria?

The concept of 'criterion' in this context needs further examination. A criterion might be highly specific and it might be important, given the purposes of the assessment, that this specific criterion be separately tested. Thus, an airline pilot would have to demonstrate ability to perform safe landings, and if he or she could not satisfy this criterion the weakness could not be compensated by flawless take-offs and a high level of navigation skills. For a broader criterion however, and in a different context, such specificity would not be relevant. Thus, for knowledge and appreciation of nineteenth century English novelists, a poor essay on a novel by Dickens could be overlooked in the light of several excellent essays about other novelists. The criterion-referenced notion needs to be expanded to deal with such complications.

Most traditional tests in England, such as GCSE examinations and typical school tests are collections of potentially criterion-referenced items for which the results are aggregated and interpreted mainly as normative scores. Thus, Grade C in history, or 54 per cent in a typical school French test, are results which have no clear meaning in terms of particular weaknesses or strengths in learning — and they are therefore of little formative value. Here again it is hard to see how the idea of criterion-referencing can apply without further development and it is to this problem that the next sections will turn.

Domain Referencing

Defining a Domain

J.W. Popham (1978), who was one of the first to develop the concept of criterion-referencing, defined it as follows:

> A criterion-referenced test is used to ascertain an individual's status with respect to a well-defined behavioural domain. (p. 93)

He introduced the notion of a domain and of 'domain-referencing' in part to clear up confusions about the concept of criterion-referencing. In common usage, as the last paragraphs of the previous section have shown, it is the operation of criteria over a range of specifics which is important. Popham took the view that domain-referencing was the only clear way to express the criterion concept. Others have taken it to be only one of several possible interpretations. The following discussion will bring out some of the issues involved in the shift from 'criterion' to 'domain'.

Any test is designed to measure a candidate's attainment in something. It could be:

- physics,
- knowledge of history,
- constitutional history of England in the sixteenth century,
- ability to design investigations to investigate the refraction of light.

These four specifications are very different from one another. 'Physics' is very broad in that it spans an enormous subject and a whole range of levels and types of attainment; 'knowledge of history' is equally broad in scope of the subject, but is delimited by the specification of knowledge. The third example delimits the history to a particular aspect of a limited period, but by omitting the word knowledge leaves open again the range of ways that a learner may be able to address issues about this aspect of this period. The last example is specific both in the topic area and in respect of the skill to be displayed in action in that area.

Each of these four phrases defines a domain. A test constructor has to start with a definition of the domain to be tested, and the outcome of the test will be interpreted as a measure of attainment in that domain. If the domain is a very wide one, then the test constructor may have to point out that the task is impossible. For the domain specified only as 'physics' any test set in a finite time could only test a small fraction of the content and skills that characterize expertise in physics. With such a small fraction, it would not be legitimate to claim that the result is a measure of attainment in physics. The task would be more manageable with a definition such as the fourth of the above list. The syllabuses set for public examinations serve to define the domains that they will test, and thereby should underpin the significance of the test results.

Specifying Cognitive Demand

The definition of a domain can only be adequately specific if it can express the boundaries, both of the content and of the ways in which this content is to be expressed, or manipulated, or put to use by a candidate. This task received an important impetus from Benjamin Bloom when in 1956 he published his *Taxonomy of Educational Objectives*. His analysis was based upon, and is illustrated by, the production and investigation of different questions and the cognitive demands that they might make of a candidate. His taxonomy comprises six levels of educational objectives that questions might aim to test: Knowledge, Comprehension, Application, Analysis, Synthesis, Evaluation. Thus a question asking for a list of events in a story would be in the Knowledge category, one that asked for description of the main idea behind a story would be Application, whilst one that asked for a critical opinion about the quality of the writing in the story would be Evaluation. The six levels were designed to form a hierarchy, in that the later categories are more demanding than the earlier ones and include and assume them (e.g. Synthesis is not feasible without prior Comprehension).

The scheme has been adapted in many ways and has been used in GCE and GCSE examinations: a typical syllabus will spell out a set of objectives, and then set these out in the form of a two dimensional grid of the content topics against the objectives. For example, 5 per cent of the total in a physics examination may be allotted to questions or parts of questions which call for comprehension (the objectives dimension) of the concepts of electrical voltage (the content dimension). This 5 per cent figure will be inserted in the cell of the grid at which 'comprehension' and 'voltage' intersect.

However, there have been many criticisms of the Bloom scheme. Some would not accept that the later levels will necessarily be more demanding than the earlier ones — a complex comprehension question could be more demanding than an analysis question on the same topic. Attempts that have been made to check the claim that the six levels are distinct and form a hierarchy have failed to support the structure — all that survives such empirical investigation is that there is a broad distinction between Knowledge on the one hand and higher order skills represented by Synthesis and Evaluation on the other. There is little basis either, for the claims about hierarchy, from the field of cognitive psychology. Not surprisingly, examiners in practice find it hard to predict what 'level' of thinking a given question will elicit, and even harder to justify the prediction when they study the many ways in which different candidates actually respond.

Some Examples

The problem of specifying a domain in terms of content and cognitive skills also encounters other difficulties when questions are being composed and trialled. From the testing perspective, the domain has to be seen as the collection of all possible questions that could be set to assess the knowledge and skills specified by the syllabus. The difficulties are illustrated by the example in *Table 1* — a question taken from the science survey tests of the APU (Black, 1990). This question was designed as one of the questions in a domain defined as 'Seeing patterns in observations'. Other questions in the same domain differed from it in several respects. Some were similar in the structure of the table of data, but dealt with quite different contexts. The performance of the same pupil could differ widely between such questions — one reason for this being that through the eyes of many pupils this would be seen as a question about agriculture rather than one about the abstract issue of patterns in observations. Some again differed in presenting the figures in order of size, for example, with USA first and Ceylon last in the above example, and not in random order, or in presenting two sets of data with a direct relationship rather than a reciprocal one; both of these variations would make the question more easy. Again, such a question could contain three columns of data, such that a clear relationship could be inferred between two sets but with no relationship of either to the third.

Table 1: *Country energy*
Records are kept of the total amount of energy a country uses each year (from oil, coal, etc).
From this the average amount used by each person in that country can be worked out.

The table below shows the percentage of the population working in agriculture and the amount of energy used per person each year for six different countries.
Describe what the table shows about the way the percentage of people working in agriculture relates to the amount of energy used per person in a country.

Country	% of population working in agriculture	Amount of energy used per person (units of energy per year)
Ceylon	50	0.8
Cuba	42	5.1
France	26	19.5
Italy	31	8.4
USA	12	66.0
W. Germany	23	26.8

Faced with evidence of the ways in which scores vary across such variations in the questions, there are two possible responses. The first is to define the domain more narrowly — which would narrow the range of attainment that the tests would measure. The other would be to include questions of all types of data presentation and over many different contexts and then sample from this domain for any particular test. The problem would then be to decide how large a sample would have to be used. A way to decide this would be to set large numbers of such questions to a representative sample of pupils and then to analyse the variations amongst the scores to determine how large a number would be needed to reduce the variability of the overall score to within tolerable limits. Only when this has been done is it possible to generalize from the results — i.e. to assert that a score (say) of 60 per cent on this particular set of questions is, within a given range of variation (for example, plus or minus 5 per cent), the score the candidate would always get on any other equally large sample of questions from this domain.

This is a formidable undertaking. The APU science project found that in order to obtain generalizable results in each of several categories of science performance that they had set out to measure, they needed about thirty-five hours of testing in order to set enough questions. This was feasible in sample surveys where each pupil need only attempt a fraction of the total tests to be administered — it would not be possible if a full set of results were needed for each pupil.

Defining, Testing, Interpreting

This discussion raises three requirements that are important in domain referencing, as follows:

- The definition of a domain has to be in terms of rules that will guide test constructors — and which will therefore have to be explicit. These rules will have to include both rules about the knowledge and skills and rules about the forms of items, for to introduce new forms is as likely to lead to new variability as the introduction of new content.
- The length of a test is closely related to the reliability with which its result can be said to represent attainment within a given domain. The APU results presented above, and research that has explored the generalizability of pupils' performances on scientific investigation problems (Shavelson *et al.*, 1993), both bear on this issue, and both show that the testing needed would be too lengthy for any externally applied system designed for all pupils. A similar conclusion emerged from research which has shown that a minimum of

thirteen different assignments were needed to obtain a satisfactory measure of writing achievement (Lehmann, 1990). The remarks of Christie, quoted in Chapter 4, are also relevant here. It need only be noted here that the breadth or narrowness of the definition of the domain, and the precision with which that is so defined can be selectively addressed in test items, both determine the severity of this problem.

- The meaning of the test result derives from the definition of the domain, and where the meaning of a test result is to be understood in this way, it is said to be domain referenced. For a test which has used an adequate sample of a given domain, the result can be generalized to mean that the candidate has a given level of attainment within the field of knowledge and skills that the domain definition describes. As Wood (1991) puts it: 'The proportion of items in a sample a person gets correct is an estimate of the proportion he would get correct if he answered every item in the universe' (p. 5).

The process by which a domain is defined, and by which the means to test it adequately are determined, is in part an empirical one. An *a priori* definition may often run into difficulties when attempts are made to operationalize it in explicit questions or other assessment procedures. There may then be a process of iteration between the definition and the attempts to mirror that definition in a set of questions. The iteration may develop further when pupils attempt such questions, for their responses may be unexpected and may throw new light on ambiguities or unexpected implications of the original conceptualisation of the domain. When all such matters are resolved, it will then be necessary to explore empirically the range of variation in pupils' responses over samples of the questions which have come to represent the domain.

An example of such iteration occurred in the development of APU science survey questions. One of the categories of science performance which was given priority by science educators was 'Observation'. Tests for this category were intended to be tests of a skill, and not tests of conceptual understanding. It was not difficult to set questions, using diagrams, photographs, and collections of natural objects and of artefacts, and to ask pupils about their recognition of particular features and of similarities and differences. However, problems arose when pupils' responses were studied. Many would observe details, e.g. amongst a collection of sea shells, which were irrelevant to the task of scientific classification. The survey team disagreed amongst themselves — some saying that as evidence of the skill of observation, such responses were as valid as the responses originally expected, others arguing that from a scientific point of view the observations were irrelevant and therefore worthless. The domain was later re-defined as 'scientific observation', but this raised problems because it was inconsistent with the attempt to achieve independence from conceptual understanding. The debate was still evolving when the surveys came to an end — its epitaph was expressed as follows in a final report:

> Thus while making and interpreting observations is included for testing in the APU science framework of scientific activity categories, it may well be that the appropriate place for its specific inclusion in taught science is a practical test closely related to the pupils' conceptual knowledge base. (Archenhold *et al.*, 1988, p. 63)

By contrast, the definition of a domain may be a topic for conceptual and ideological battles. Notable examples are the domains of literacy, a term which has a plethora of meanings (McLean, 1990), and of reading, where controversies over appropriate testing methods are intertwined with differences in the conceptualisation of the 'skill' (Gipps and Stobart, 1993, pp. 67–9).

Such problems are all entailed in the definition of Popham (1978) quoted above — the phrase 'a well-defined behavioural domain' can be unwrapped to open up a Pandora's box of problems in test construction and interpretation. The concept of 'domain-referencing' is clearly appropriate to any consideration of the meaning of GCSE and most school examinations. However, few would claim that these work with and reflect 'well-defined behavioural domains'. In public examinations, there are serious attempts to delimit the knowledge and skills, but little attention has been given to the problems of the variability arising from different forms of question presentation.

Where the domains are very broad, the claim that the score does represent what would have been obtained by an attempt at every item in the universe is hard to sustain. Even if it could be, the information might lack educational value because so many different patterns of strengths and weaknesses could be implied by the same total score. A possible improvement here would be to divide up the domain into a number of distinct and educationally significant component domains. Then the testing, the scoring and the reporting would produce a profile of performances, i.e. a set of scores each representing a different component of the original domain. The national curriculum assessment in England was originally designed to yield a profile across such components. However, the results are now collapsed to yield only a single result over those targets being externally assessed — the remnants of a profile still exist only insofar as those components which are only assessed by teachers' assessments are reported separately. The reason for the collapsing was a general one — to test several sub-domains with adequate reliability requires more time and other expense than to test the collection as a single whole. Thus manageability and economy were improved — but the price paid was a loss of meaning.

Rules or Judgments?

A practical difficulty with criterion or domain referencing is that it is not possible to define every component in a domain with such explicit precision that a given test item, or a given piece of work by a pupil, can be assessed as meeting the requirements of the domain. There is a temptation to achieve precision by attempting to define every aim in atomized forms — this can lead to the production of large numbers of very specific test items, which may well be invalid because each atomized piece is tested out of context. Further problems will also follow in deciding how to aggregate the large and uneven collections of results that any one pupil attains. A more robust approach is outlined by Popham (1993) in his discussion of this problem:

> In today's educational setting, with high-stakes tests and attendant pressures on teachers to boost students' test scores, we dare not build tests that incline teachers to short-change students by teaching only to narrow non-generalisable targets. Nor dare we return to the era when amorphous norm-referenced test specifications ruled the realm.

> The key elements of this form of criterion referenced test-item specifications are (1) a brief *verbal description* of the skill or knowledge being assessed and (2) several *illustrative items* that might be employed for assessment purposes. The verbal description must capture the intellectual essence of that which is to be assessed.

> The illustrative items should assist teachers to understand what is being assessed, but these items should not exhaust the potential types of items that might be used.

There is no escape from the need for professional judgment in setting up the definitions of the domain and in judging any particular piece of work in relation to that definition. Attempts to set up explicit rules so that expert judgment is not required are bound to fail.

Aggregation, Profiles and Progress

Dividing a Domain According to Content

As emphasized above, there is an inevitable loss of meaning when scores are aggregated. Numerical scores assigned to a pupil by the application of a marking scheme to his or her assessment responses can have a misleading appearance of significant meaning. It can be misleading because it hides the fact that the final number may represent the sum of judgments on very diverse performances, so that the addition of numbers from the component marks is as suspect as an attempt to add together a measure of one's weight, the price of bread and the smell of a rose i.e. it would be hard to justify treating these numbers as if they were measures on the same scale. As Hoffman (1978) puts it:

> To compress all our information about a single candidate into a single ranking number is clearly absurd — quite ridiculously irrational. And yet it has to be done. (p. 35)

Whilst the 'absurdity' cannot be escaped, the gap between a score or grade and rational meaning can be narrowed by sub-dividing a domain. There are two possible approaches to the task of sub-division The first has already been discussed: the domain can be divided into component areas of knowledge and skills and the component scores used to report a profile of performances. It would still be the case that any component score would involve a generalization over two aspects. One could imagine that all of the questions involved were of the same kind and difficulty, and differed only in testing the appropriate contents and skills. In that case, a score of 45 per cent would imply success over 45 per cent of the range of the component domain. Alternatively, the questions could cover a very narrow range but might vary in difficulty. In that case, the 45 per cent could imply a position on a scale ranging from perfect understanding to complete incomprehension. In most real examples, the questions will inevitably cover a range of levels of difficulty as well as a range of the domain content, and it may not make sense to talk of unravelling the two. However, this discussion leads in to the next section, which considers a different approach to sub-dividing a domain.

Dividing a Domain According to Models of Progression

The problems can be seen in a different way if the assessment is conducted in the light of a model of progression in the learning of a domain. A cognitive analysis could place the universe of questions into an ordered sequence, which might be justified in terms of a theory of the learning of the domain, or empirically, or by a combination of the two. The sequence may imply a hierarchy of dependence in that the learning of the easier items could be an essential requirement for the learning of later ones. Insofar as such a sequence could be well grounded empirically, the marking could then be designed so that a score such as 45 per cent could be interpreted as achievement of successful learning up to a given level in this sequence. It is most unlikely that pupils would perform as consistently as any tightly drawn recipe for progression might require. However, it could be possible to identify questions at which the pupil showed very high success, those at which there was hardly any success, and those where there was a partial success but with significant imperfections. The attainment might then be judged to be in the range covered by the partially achieved items (Brown and Denvir, 1987; Masters and Evans, 1986).

Such an interpretation could hardly be achieved unless the questions had been carefully trialled and selected with some model of progression in mind. Attempts to impose an interpretation of 'progress' on a collection of scores for a set of questions that have not been developed with this purpose in mind have often failed. Pupils appear inconsistent — some achieving modest scores by gaining high marks on the harder items whilst failing on those that are more generally easy, others doing the opposite.

The public examinations taken at age 16 in England were always loosely related to criteria through the examination syllabuses, but it has never been possible to match the grades awarded to a set of performance descriptions appropriate to each grade except in a very general way. Loosely formulated grade descriptions have been used for many years, but more rigorous attempts were made following a government commitment made in 1984 in relation to the new GCSE examination coming in 1988. It was stated that:

> . . . examination grades should have a clearer meaning and pupils and teachers need clearer goals. We accordingly need grade-related criteria which will specify the knowledge, understanding and skills expected for the award of particular grades. (Gipps and Stobart, 1993, p. 77)

Where this was tried by *post hoc* analysis from existing papers the attempt failed for the reason given above. Groups also tried to draw up collections of grade-related criteria for several subjects on an *a priori* basis — but the specifications became so lengthy and detailed that there were fears that they would act as a straitjacket on the examining system. A different more inductive exercise was then started working from existing practice in particular syllabuses, but this was suspended with the coming of national assessment.

A different attempt was made in the TGAT plans for national assessment, which recommended that the national curriculum should be set out to specify the expected progression in learning in a set of ten levels. National assessment would then be designed to produce a level assignment as the record of attainment of each pupil. One reason for this was the need to have a single consistent scheme to apply to assessments of pupils from ages 7 to 16. This plan ran into problems. Each level description was inevitably a collection of many different features of performance and there was no time to test these out by empirical research. At first, the testing approach was to separately test for each level with as many different specific items as possible, thus leading to collections of highly specific questions, and complex rules to determine on how many of the questions for any one level a pupil should succeed in order to achieve that level. Subsequently, when the system was extensively revised in 1994, the status of the ten-level system was changed by stating that it was for assessment purposes only and not to guide learning, and the level criteria were set out in more general terms. This could have been the beginning of an attempt to follow the advice of Popham quoted above. However, practice at present appears to be to assign levels on the basis of total scores on a collection of questions that span the level: thus the criterion basis is a weak one.

Measuring Progress

Three underlying problems haunt attempts of this kind, as follows:

- Adequate descriptions of the domain or domains concerned, grounded in clear theoretical models and supported by adequate empirical evidence, are rarely formulated. This fault is particularly serious in relationship to attempts to set up and assess any coherent scheme of progression in learning.
- Aggregation over scores from diverse questions can give meaningless totals. This can be tackled first by limiting the range of content in a domain. It can also be eased, in relation to recording progression, by limiting the range of difficulty. This might require the setting of tests of different levels of 'progress' or 'difficulty' and using the limited testing time available for pupils by assigning each to the particular test which covers the level or levels to which he or she is already reported to have progressed. The sets of tiered tests used in national curriculum assessment are examples of this approach.
- It is difficult to decide upon the criterion scores required to achieve a given level in a scheme of progression. This difficulty is discussed in the next section.

The dimension of progression in learning has a particular importance in relation to a different aspect of score referencing, called ipsative referencing. The term 'ipsative' appears to have been invented for the purpose, deriving from the Latin 'ipse' for self. The principle here is that an individual's performance in a particular domain at a given time is to be judged in relation to his or her other performances. These could be performances in the same domain on previous occasions — comparison which would be the more informative insofar as the indicators of past performance bore some meaningful relationship to present achievements. The comparison could be across different domains at a particular time, thus giving a personal profile. For the purposes of formative assessment, and particularly where self assessment by pupils is to be emphasized, an ipsative focus for assessment would seem valuable, but it has received little attention since it was introduced in 1944 by Cattell. As for the other varieties of referencing, it is a particular perspective of interpretation rather than an alternative: a personal 'ipsative profile' for example could hardly be considered without reference to the norm and criterion interpretation of its component scores or grades.

Grades, Cut Scores and Standards

From Marks to Grades

The discussion above has already shifted to and fro between numerical marks and their interpretation in terms of grades. The change from one to the other can have important implications. For example, where scores on an examination such as the GCSE vary from one year to the next, it is hard to judge whether any changes are due to changes in the difficulty of the questions, or to changes in the severity of the marking schemes, or to changes in the learning achievements of the candidates. The reporting of results in grades is in part an attempt to overcome some of the problems. Examiners try to establish by their own judgment a consistency for the performance at (say) the borderline between grades C and D in GCSE. The distributions of marks gained over all the entrants will be one piece of evidence, but the examiners' familiarity with the questions, with the marking schemes and with samples of pupils' responses will also be taken into account. Such exercise of judgment has been called 'construct-referenced' assessment — it relies upon the ideas and values in the heads of the examiners. In this approach, the total raw mark which specifies (for example) the lower borderline of grade C might well vary from year to year. It could be that the use of expert judgment in this way is the optimum policy, but it then makes it very difficult to defend the outcomes if critics who will not trust the judgment of examiners call in question any changes in the rates of success.

The problem of determining such grade boundary or 'cut scores' is common across many types of assessment and testing (Gipps and Stobart, 1993, pp. 93–6). It is a problem in which two features are inter-twined, namely the shared understanding of domain performance criteria and the judgment of specific samples of work in terms of these criteria. Attempts have been made to make the process rather less subjective than the GCSE practice described above. Where the purpose of a test is to select for a limited and fixed number of places, the problem is simply solved. If there are N places, the first N candidates succeed. A more refined approach would look at the predictive use of the test results, and ask experts to judge the score which would minimize the proportions of wrong predictions — as might be the case for A-level students predicted as likely to be successful in a degree course.

A different and more general approach, proposed by Angoff (1971), relates the process directly to domain criteria. Each of a set of experts is asked to make a judgment on every item in a multiple choice test (the procedure can readily be adapted to other types of test). The judgment required is the expert's estimate of the proportion of those who, being on the borderline of achievement of the criterion, would get the item right. The sum of these probabilities over the items will give an estimate of the cut score, and these will be averaged over all the experts provided that the differences between them are not too great. As for the GCSE procedure, the hope is that negotiated agreements between experts will transcend subjectivity. It follows that such procedures must introduce a degree of unreliability into the process, because there is bound to be some variability in the agreed judgments (Cresswell, 1996). This unreliability adds some error to graded results, over and above the errors due to unreliability in the original scores.

Dangerous Simplifications

For the purposes of public reporting of results, the judgment of a cut score may be for a grade, or for attestation of basic or minimum competency, for assurance that a certain 'standard' has been attained. The process therefore becomes a key move in relation to the public accountability of educational systems. Whilst public opinion, reflected, assisted or provoked by political leaders and the media, rightly demands some measure of educational performance, it cannot cope with the complexity that any authentic picture of human performances should portray. The necessary simplifications are to be achieved through a simplified language which rests on the interpretations of the results of assessment and testing. In this language, the word 'standards' is in common use. It applies over all spheres of public life with the implication, to quote a dictionary, that it means 'the degree of excellence etc. required for a particular purpose'.

One vision for monitoring the improvement of education is that national 'standards' will be established through a specified curriculum with performance criteria, and then achievement of these 'standards' will be checked by testing. In the light of this purpose, the definition proposed by Wiliam (1996a) is appropriate:

> Within this view, a 'standard', then, is simply a level of performance which is equated with a point on a score scale for which particular meanings are sought, and the validation of the standard setting procedure consists in showing that this equation is justified. (p. 290)

Wiliam goes on to point out that the score itself is arbitrary in the sense that it depends on examiners' judgments in establishing and interpreting a mark scheme. The selection of the appropriate level also involves judgement, and for policy purposes there are difficult trade-offs entailed. For example, if the level were set at (say) 70 per cent correct then perhaps 85 per cent of students would achieve and the 85 per cent could be proclaimed a high standard; however, only 60 per cent might achieve if the standard were set at 90 per cent correct — but the 90 per cent could then be proclaimed as the high standard. This ambiguity has been evident in the UK — those suspicious of a rise in GCSE pass rates may assert that 'standards' have fallen, their reference being to the level set for success, others make reference to the numbers or proportions reaching this criterion level, so that if GCSE pass rates were to fall the effect would also be deplored as a fall in 'standards' (Wiliam, 1996b). Thus the standards enterprise has to confront all of the problems of domain specification, aggregation of scores, and cut score determination, that are outlined above, and so the standards debates do not raise any fundamentally new issues of principle in assessment. Nevertheless, in political and policy debates, the term is widely used and the meanings that it conveys and develops are of great importance.

A more subtle ambiguity in these debates is worthy of attention. Where minimum or basic competence is at issue, it would seem to follow that success must be achieved in all components, so that there can be no trade-offs between weak performance in one aspect and high scores in another. If a domain can be divided up into a set of explicitly defined performances then testing for success in each and every performance is relatively straightforward. Where, as is more usual, there is a set of multi-purpose domains such as 'basic literacy' and 'basic numeracy' then all of the problems are encountered again, becoming more severe as the breadth of the domains and the sweep of generalizability of any results are increased.

Ambiguous Hopes

National debates about standards also tend to be ambiguous between minima and scales. For example, the national curriculum in England sets out standards in terms of a set of levels and the nation's progress will be discussed in terms of the distribution of attainments across these levels. The TGAT report specified that level 2 should be fixed at the best estimate of the norm expectation for the average 7-year old, level 3 for the 9-year old, level 4 for the 11-year old and so on (the interplay here of criterion and norm referencing is typical and inevitable). Given this, it would follow that at (say) age 11 there would be a distribution of performances with the mean at level 4. However, some commentators and critics have since discussed results of testing at age 11 as if level 4 were a base-line which all should achieve, and have therefore deplored the significant proportion of pupils who do not attain it by age 11, despite the fact that this result was an inevitable consequence of the way in which the level criteria were determined. This slide, from a mean to a minimum, frequently occurs in discussion about standards.

It is also possible for a national standards specification to seem to ignore this issue. The USA document on national standards for science education specifies that it is setting out standards for all to attain and gives no indication of a scale, or a set of levels, or a set of grades. The implication is that minimum competency for all is being described, yet the document reads more like a description of a range of achievements which it would be ambitious to expect from the average pupil. The reason for this may be that this is a national document with no legislative power (control being in the hands of the fifty states) and can only be influential insofar as it encourages those with the power to aim higher and in the 'right' direction. Thus it has to be challenging, and also supportive of improvement programmes. To start inserting qualifications about varieties of performance would be to weaken this challenge and even to seem to excuse mediocrity. Here, the rhetorical requirements have been judged to be more important than practical and technical realities. That this could be the correct strategy serves to illustrate how standards debates are to be judged in the context of their function in public discourses of influence, and not solely in terms of their technical grounding. Thus the formulation of a standard may be judged in terms of its effects, in this case the feedback effect on teaching and learning, and this may justify the formulation in accordance with the general concept of consequential validity. Debates on standards should concentrate on their effects on the systems in which they are formulated.

What Makes Assessment Results Meaningful?

It should now be clear that the various approaches discussed — normative, criterion, domain and ipsative referencing — are interlinked and overlaid in any practical assessment procedure. Their theoretical value is as conceptual tools to identify and describe the ways in which different systems operate rather than as distinct categories within which any one system can be uniquely classified.

It should also be clear that the interpretation of any assessment or test result depends on the domain definition, on the scoring schemes and the procedures for determining grade boundaries or cut scores, and on the referencing system in relation to which any scores or grades are meant to be interpreted. Issues of reliability and validity have also lurked behind much of the discussion. All scores and boundary decisions have to be interpreted in terms of the errors inherent in the measurements on which they are based. The performance on a set of items only relates to the domain definition if the test instruments have content and construct validity. The cut scores, grades or interpretations in terms of standards may also depend on the consequential validity — for example, in any framework of minimum competence.

Thus, whilst all of these issues can be discussed in isolation for the purposes of explanation, they are all in play simultaneously in the design and operation of a testing system, and their interplay has to be tuned and judged in relation to the single or multiple purposes that the system is meant to serve.

Summary

- The meaning of an individual test score may be determined by norm referencing, i.e. by relating it to the scores of others.
- Standardized tests are designed to measure well defined constructs and to give scores which are interpretable in relation to population norms.
- A different way to assign meaning is to link scores to the achievement of defined criteria.
- In practice, criteria relate to performance over a given domain of knowledge and skills, which always involves generalization derived from a set of specific performances.
- A number of questions, covering ranges of content, difficulty and question types may be needed to produce a fair representation of a domain.
- A profile of scores relating to a set of sub-domains may be more informative than a single overall domain score, but it will also be more costly to produce.
- Domains may be sub-divided according to a model of progression in learning, but it is difficult to validate such schemes in practice.
- Interpretation of marks to assign grades can be done by reference to norms or to criteria; common practice seems to use a mixture of both approaches.
- Decisions about criteria, and in particular the setting of cut-scores, cannot be achieved by automatic rules — there is no substitute for expert judgment.
- The term 'standards' is much favoured in public debate but is open to several interpretations and can thereby generate ambiguity.

Bibliography

AIRASIAN, P.W. (1991) *Classroom Assessment*, New York: McGraw Hill. Chapter 8.
BROWN, S. (1981) *What Do They Know? A Review of Criterion-Referenced Assessment*, Edinburgh: HMSO. A very thorough discussion of the principles covering the literature up to 1980.

CROCKER, L. and ALGINA, J. (1986) *An Introduction to Classical and Modern Test Theory*, New York: Holt, Rinehart and Winston. Chapter 4 for domain sampling and Chapters 18 and 19 for cut scores and standard setting.

GIPPS, C. (1994) *Beyond Testing: Towards a Theory of Educational Assessment.* London: Falmer Press, Chapter 5.

GIPPS, C.V. and STOBART, G. (1993) *Assessment. A Teachers' Guide to the Issues,* London: Hodder and Stoughton. Chapters 3, 7 and 8, particularly for GCSE and National Curriculum issues in England.

HANNA, G.S. (1993) *Better Teaching Through Better Measurement,* Orlando FL: Harcourt Bruce. Chapters 16 to 19 and Appendices A and B for use of standardized tests.

OECD (1995) *Performance Standards in Education. In Search of Quality.* Paris: OECD. Authors from ten countries each describe their country's debates about standards.

SALVIA, J. and YSSELDYKE, J.E. (1991) *Assessment,* Boston: Houghton Mifflin. Chapters 2 and 6 on general issues and on norm referencing, Chapters 4 and 5 for basic statistics, plus most chapters from Chapter 9 onwards for detailed discussion of the uses of standardized tests.

STIGGINS, R.J. (1994) *Student-Centered Classroom Assessment,* New York: Merrill/Macmillan. Chapters 4 and 13.

WOOD, R. (1991) *Assessment and Testing,* Cambridge: Cambridge University Press. Chapter 7.

References

ANGOFF, W.H. (1971) 'Norms, scales and equivalent scores', in THORNDIKE, R.L. (ed.) *Educational Measurement,* 2nd edition, Washington DC: American Council on Education.

ARCHENHOLD, W.F., BELL, J.F., DONNELLY, J., JOHNSON, S. and WELFORD, G. (1988) *Science at Age 15: A Review of APU Findings 1980–84,* London: HMSO.

BLACK, P.J. (1990) 'APU science — the past and the future', *School Science Review,* **72**, 258, pp. 13–28.

BLOOM, B.S., ENGELHART, M.D., FURST, E.J., HILL, W.H. and KRATHWOHL, D.R. (1956) *Taxonomy of Educational Objectives. Handbook 1: Cognitive Domain,* New York: David McKay.

BROWN, M. and DENVIR, B. (1987) 'The feasibility of class administered diagnostic assessment in primary mathematics', *Educational Research,* **29**, 2, pp. 95–107.

BUROS, I.K. (each year) *Mental Measurements Year Book,* Highland Park NJ: Gryphon.

CATTELL, R.B. (1944) 'Psychological measurement: Normative, ipsative, interactive', *Psychological Review,* **51**, pp. 292–303.

CRESWELL, M.J. (1996) 'Defining, setting and maintaining standards in curriculum-embedded examinations: Judgemental and statistical approaches', in GOLDSTEIN, H. and LEWIS, T. (eds) *Assessment: Problems, Developments and Statistical Issues,* Chichester and New York: John Wiley, see p. 63, pp. 57–84.

GIPPS, C. and STOBART, G. (1993) *Assessment. A Teachers' Guide to the Issues,* London: Hodder and Stoughton.

HANNA, G.S. (1993) *Better Teaching Through Better Measurement*, Orlando: Harcourt Brace.

HOFFMAN, B. (1978) *The Tyranny of Testing*, New York: Greenwood Press.

LEHMANN, R.H. (1990) 'Reliability and generalizability of ratings of compositions', *Studies in Educational Evaluation*, **16**, pp. 501–12.

LEVY, P. and GOLDSTEIN, H. (eds) (1984) *Tests in Education: A Book of Critical Reviews*, London: Academic Press.

LINN, R.L. (1994) *Assessment Based Reform: Challenges to Educational Measurement*, Angoff Memorial Lecture, Princeton, NJ: Educational Testing Service.

LINN, R.L., GRAUE, E. and SANDERS, N.M. (1990) 'Comparing state and district test results to national norms: The validity of claims that "Everyone is above average"', *Educational Measurement: Issues and Practice*, **9**, 3, pp. 5–14.

MASTERS, G.N. and EVANS, J. (1986) 'A sense of direction in criterion referenced assessment', *Studies in Educational Evaluation*, **12**, pp. 257–65.

McLEAN, L. (1990) 'Possibilities and limitations in cross-national comparisons of educational achievement', in BROADFOOT, P., MURPHY, R. and TORRANCE, H. (eds) *Changing Educational Assessment: International Perspectives and Trends*, London: Routledge, pp. 65–77.

POPHAM, W.J. (1978) *Criterion-referenced Measurement*, Englewood Cliffs, NJ: Prentice Hall.

POPHAM, W.J. (1993) *Educational Evaluation*, 3rd edition, Boston: Alleyn and Bacon.

SHAVELSON, R.J., BAXTER, G.P. and GAO, X. (1993) 'Sampling variability of performance assessments', *Journal of Educational Measurement*, **30**, 3, pp. 215–32.

WILIAM, D. (1996a) 'Meanings and consequences in standard setting', *Assessment in Education*, **3**, 3, pp. 287–307.

WILIAM, D. (1996b) 'Standards in examinations: A matter of trust?', *The Curriculum Journal*, **7**, 3, pp. 293–306.

WOOD, R. (1991) *Assessment and Testing*, Cambridge: Cambridge University Press.

Chapter 6

How to Assess — Methods and Instruments

A Tool Box

There is a wide range of methods available to assess the learning perform-ance of pupils. The choice amongst these will be made in the light of their fitness for the purpose of the assessment, constrained by issues of practical-ity — notably limitations of time and expense. The purpose of this chapter is to describe this range of methods, with emphases on their fitness for purposes and on their practicality.

This chapter cannot serve as a guide to the composition of good ques-tions and other assessment exercises — some indication of sources for such guidance is given in the bibliography. The account will have to be a rather general one, bereft of examples, with the aim of providing a comprehensive overview of the field. It should serve as an introduction for the critical user and for illuminating the problems of the design of assessment systems which are discussed further in Chapter 9.

The structure of the presentation will at first follow the notion of a spectrum of methods, ranging from those where the response is tightly con-strained, as in multiple choice questions, to those where response is open, as in essays or investigation projects. This sequence will then be followed by a section on systems in which these methods are collected and combined, and a section on issues to do with preparation and analysis of tests.

Fixed Response

The common form used here is the multiple-choice test, which is made up of a stem and a set of options from which the pupil has to choose. There are many variants: two common examples are true/false questions and matching questions. A true/false question can be classified as a particular type of two option multiple choice. An example of a matching question would be to ask the pupil to select from a list of five scientists the ones who made each of four well-known discoveries. Such questions can be designed to test knowledge, reasoning which can lead to a single correct answer, and some procedural skills.

There are several well documented rules to guide the construction of such questions (Stiggins, 1994, Chapter 6; Airasian, 1991, Chapter 6; Millman and Greene, 1989, p. 353). The stem should ask a single clearly focused question using language well within the reading level of the pupils. Negatives should be avoided. Diagrams and pictures can be an economical way of setting out the question situation. A complex or lengthy stem can be justified if it can serve as the basis for several questions. The options should all be similar to one another in numbers of words and style, both for directness and to avoid giving clues, whether genuine or false. Questions should be checked by several experts, in part to ensure that there are no circumstances or legitimate reasoning by virtue of which any of the distracters (the options designed to be incorrect) could be correct, in part to look for unintended clues to the correct option, in part to ensure that this option really is correct. The main challenge in setting good questions is to ensure that the distracters are plausible — but not too plausible — so that they represent a significant challenge to the pupil's knowledge and understanding.

There are complicated arguments in the literature about the best number of options (Wood, 1991, p. 39). The most common practice is to use four or five (i.e. one key — correct — and three or four distracters). Since most analyses show that a change from four to five makes little difference either to pupils' results or to the overall quality of a test, it is usually advisable to keep with four, if only for the reason that with every extra distracter it becomes increasingly difficult to ensure comparability with the others in both wording and plausibility. *In extremis*, the tired inventor may be tempted to use 'none of the above' as the last of the set — this should be avoided, for where it is the key, it makes the question very difficult as the pupil has to be sure that all of the others are wrong.

It is always possible to guess at an answer, and a completely ignorant pupil can score 25 per cent by random guessing in a test with four option items. However, whilst it is possible to set up simple formulae to 'correct' for this effect by subtracting from the total correct a number based on the number of wrong answers, this is not usually done. It turns out to have very little effect on the overall rank order of scores. It is also doubtful that more than a few pupils would guess completely at random, and it is hard to formulate the best advice to give a pupil when such a correction is to be applied ('If you are more than 50 per cent certain that one of two of the options is correct, then . . .').

A sophistication of the normal multiple-choice test is available through the use of computer adaptive testing. Here, the questions to be presented to a pupil at any point during a test can be chosen on the basis of the quality of the answers supplied up to that point. This can mean that each pupil can avoid spending time on items which give little useful information because they are far too hard or far too easy for her (Bunderson *et al.*, 1989).

The advantages of fixed response questions can be summarized as follows:

- Because of the large number of such items which pupils can attempt in a given testing time, they can achieve greater coverage and greater overall reliability than is possible with other types of question.
- Pupils' achievements are not dependent on their writing skills.
- There is no threat to reliability in the marking.
- Because a multiple choice test yields a large number of scores on a simple scale (all 1 or 0), statistical analysis of the scores is relatively straightforward.
- The quality can be kept high by pre-testing a larger number of items than will be needed, discarding those which seem unsuitable and modifying others.

The disadvantages of such questions are also clear:

- They can give no direct evidence of pupils' reasons for their choices, so their value for formative and diagnostic purposes is limited.
- Pupils may obtain some correct answers by guesswork.
- Some studies have shown that up to a third of pupils who choose a correct response may do so for a wrong reason (Tamir, 1990).
- The knowledge or reasoning that is tested will be in an isolated or restricted context, so that complex structures of knowledge and reasoning cannot be assessed.
- Heavy or exclusive reliance on such questions in high-stakes tests can lead to emphasis, in teaching to the test, on an atomized approach to learning and to a passivity in which one judges other people's ideas but does not propose, formulate or create ideas of one's own.
- A high level of experience and expertise is needed to set good questions of this type.

Closed Response

Questions in this and later categories may all be called 'supply items': this name captures the essential difference from the previous category, but requires supplementation to specify the extent to which what is to be supplied is constrained by the form of the question. There is a great variety here even amongst closed response questions — some common examples are:

- supply one word or short phrase answers to specific knowledge questions;

- propose words to fill the blank spaces in a set of sentences;
- supply a reason in your own words for a given event or phenomenon;
- explain the reason for your answer to a multiple choice question;
- solve a numerical problem which requires only a small number of steps;
- with a structured, multi-part presentation, require pupils to attempt a complex problem through tackling a guided sequence of component steps;
- on the basis of a supplied text or set of data, answer a set of short questions designed to test understanding of the text, or skill in responding to and handling new evidence.

Given these varieties, and there are many more, questions of this type provide a very flexible resource. They can be used to assess knowledge, reasoning and skills at various levels of complexity. They retain some of the advantages of fixed response questions in that a fair number can still be tackled in a short time; it is usual to indicate, by providing a set of blank spaces or lines, the length of answer expected. The marking can still use fairly tight schemes so that it can be reliable. The challenges set to the pupils can be far more authentic than for fixed response questions. An example would be a test of capacity to understand a new set of ideas presented in a prose passage, using a set of short answer questions which assess the pupil's understanding of the new ideas presented in the text.

Because the reasoning of the respondent can be expressed, these closed response questions are less difficult to compose because allowance can be made in the marking for some of the misunderstandings and ambiguities — i.e. those which can be seen in the response. However, the need for clear guidance and sharply focused questions remains, and ambiguity in the demand can still destroy the value of the questions. For some science tests using short open questions, Gauld (1980) found that students often misread the demand of a question, seem more incompetent than they are because they make a single slip in a complex process, fail to use what they know because they judge it irrelevant, and may be marked down because the marker cannot understand the quality of thinking behind non-standard responses.

Those questions which are based on a structured sequence have to be designed and tested out with great care. It is hard to avoid sequential effects, whereby a mistake early on can make it impossible for a pupil to gain any credit for subsequent sections, although sensitive and flexible marking can sometimes deal with this difficulty. It should also be noted that to provide such a structure makes an enormous reduction in the complexity of a problem — for in complex problems it is precisely the task of breaking up the task into a sequential strategy that is often the most demanding aspect.

Overall such questions represent the best of both worlds between fixed response and essay questions — they show many ways of compromising between the narrowness of the former and the problems that bedevil the latter.

Essay Types

The response of a pupil in composing an essay and the teacher's work in evaluating that response both take a lot of time, so it is essential that some time and care are given to composing the originating question. The topic should be one that is central to the course, and the mode of presenting the task should specify it clearly. Compare, for example, the question:

Write an essay on the applications of physics

with the following alternative:

Write an essay on the applications of physics. You should choose only one of the three main areas of physics you have studied this term — waves, dynamics, electromagnetism. For the one that you choose, describe three applications, explaining for each how it is to be understood in terms of the principles of physics and why it is of practical importance.

This second example sets out the material on which the essay is to be based, specifies the kinds of reasoning needed, and conveys ideas about the criteria which will be used in the marking. The short version would probably evoke a wide range of answers, and it would be very likely that some pupils would not do themselves justice because they would not be able to work out what exactly the examiner was looking for. In consequence, the task of marking the wide variety of answers in a fair way would be almost impossible.

There are certain verbs which are commonly used in essay questions — such as identify, describe, state, explain, compare and contrast — and the pupil has to be able to interpret these. They are often ambiguous, and their use can sometimes hide a vagueness in the examiner's own mind; thus they should only be used with some elaborating detail to explain what is intended.

The marking of essay questions can be done either using a detailed scheme or by impression marking. Whichever is used, it is helpful to have a set of qualitative criteria, better if these can be set out to give a rating scale — i.e. sets of qualitative statements which describe properties of answers, with one set for each of the marks or grades to be used to sum up the quality of the work. Many research enquiries have explored the differences between analytic or 'checklist' marking, and holist or 'impression' marking. There is no clear outcome in favour of the one or the other. What does seem clear is that the worst effects of unreliability can be avoided if there are at least two markers for every pupil response, who work independently. It is better to have two rapid markings by two independent examiners than one slower exercise by one person alone (Wood, 1991, Chapter 5).

The advantage of essay questions which call for open and extended responses is that they require complex structures of knowledge and reasoning to be explored, and they can explore the pupil's capacity to select, assemble and integrate various facets of knowledge and understanding, and to explain, evaluate, and be creative with such material. In formative assessment usage, these advantages can by enriched if the feedback to each student includes guidance on each of the dimensions of response which were judged to be important. The frequent practice, in which the busy teacher marking homework gives a mark of (say) seven out of ten without any explanatory comment, dissipates much of the potential learning value of the pupil's work.

One disadvantage is that pupils can hide uncertainty or ignorance by neglecting to address particular issues. However, the usual problem is the difficulty of ensuring that the marking is reliable. This problem has always worried examining agencies, particularly after Hartog and Rhodes (1936) showed, by experiments with multiple marking, how unreliable such marking could be. In his review of evidence, Wood (1991, Chapter 5) concludes that with only one marker, a reliability coefficient is unlikely to be greater than 0.6 — which is seriously low — and that multiple marking will help reduce this. The unreliability of a single marker can arise both from variations over time in the standards used by the marker and by departures from the common scheme of marking. However, it is hard to generalize about the seriousness of the problem — it will depend on the clarity and precision of the question, on the nature of the subject matter and on the time and effort invested in training examiners.

Most of what has been said here assumes that the essay is written under examination conditions, and thus for summative purposes. This need not be the case. The range of approaches can be expanded to include writing on the basis of library research, and writing with free access to books and notes (which can also be made available in 'Open Book' examinations). As new possibilities of this type are explored, this category of questions overlaps into the field of performance assessment, to which the discussion will now turn.

Performance Assessment

Direct Reality

It is difficult to give a precise definition to delimit the activities to be dealt with in this section. One unifying idea is that it is to do with assessment of activities which can be direct models of the reality to be assessed rather than disconnected fragments or surrogates. As Airasian (1991) puts it 'Rather than asking pupils to *tell* what they would do, performance assessment requires that they *show* what they can do' (p. 252) or, as Stiggins (1994) puts it '. . . we observe students while they are performing or we examine the products created, and we judge the level of proficiency demonstrated' (p. 160).

An example would be the skills of measurement in science. These should be assessed with a real task and require the handling of real equipment, and not, as some have tried, by an exercise on paper using pictures and diagrams of the instruments. Several attempts to check on whether such surrogates, whether on paper or by computer simulation, are valid show that they cannot be because they give results very different from performance tasks (Baxter and Shavelson, 1994). However, the notion of 'reality' is a tough one. To take the measurement example further, it has also been shown that many pupils who are competent at carrying out a specific measurement task when directed to do so will not choose to deploy this skill in a holistic investigation where they have to compose the strategy of which skilled measurement should form a part (Black, 1990). The whole investigation result would be the only valid one if the inference to be drawn was about competence in tackling investigations which might call for skill in measurement. This example raises the general issue of context–skill interaction which has already arisen in the context of the two-dimensional nature of reading skills discussed in the section on 'Validity and learning' in Chapter 4.

Much of the US literature speaks both of 'performance assessment' and of 'authentic assessment'. The general description given in Darling-Hammond *et al.* (1995) implies that authentic assessment tasks might have the following characteristics:

- you can see how students learn as well as what they have learnt;
- one tries to assess complex tasks which call for integrating knowledge;
- students are challenged to generate new knowledge and products;
- tasks call for the ability to engage in intellectual, interpersonal or intrapersonal work;
- tasks reflect the reality of the field of study being explored in the curriculum;
- tasks can last for a variety of time periods, both short and long;
- tasks are embedded in the curriculum and an assessment is made of pupils' response to a genuine learning experience, not a contrived one;
- tasks are set in real contexts that connect school work to real world experience. (pp. 3–4)

All but the last two of these are also characteristics of performance assessments, but these last two show the distinction from them. A performance assessment can be an *ad hoc* assessment exercise, whereas an 'authentic' assessment is a performance assessment in the normal learning context. The scope of activities embraced by these definitions is very wide. Performances can be in psychomotor skills, in athletics, in communication skills, in applying new concepts to extended problems, in designing and making artefacts and so on.

Choosing Tasks with Foresight

The choice of the task is a critical feature if the learning and assessment aims are to be attained. The teacher has to foresee and appraise the opportunity that the task offers for the pupils to deploy and/or develop the knowledge and skills which are the target of the assessment. This calls for a skilled and multi-dimensional foresight — constraints of time, of facilities, and of the starting-point of the pupil, have to be reckoned with. In the case of open tasks particularly, the intentions may be frustrated if the pupil's choice is guided by ignorance of, or deliberate avoidance of, some of the key concepts and skills which the task was designed to evoke. Thus, the possible responses of the pupils have to be thought through — a feat of imaginative prediction which is hard to achieve without extensive experience. An example of an attempt to provide the teacher with ideas to support wise decisions at this stage can be seen in the Nuffield curriculum materials intended to support authentic tasks in Design and Technology (Barlex *et al.*, 1995).

Any task can be specified to the pupil in a variety of ways. The degree to which the task is left open or constrained can be varied — mainly by defining more or less clearly the nature of the outcome. A pupil may be asked to design a light waterproof coat for a 4-year old; then the choice of material is part of the task, but this aspect can be altered by specifying that it must be made of a nylon fabric, thus ensuring that skill in handling this material is developed and assessed. As in setting essay tasks, the specification should set the boundaries clearly and communicate to the pupils the criteria of quality which will be used to judge the outcome. It can be important that the teacher is able, during the course of the work, to alter the specification in the light of progress. Thus, if a pupil is unable to cope with the uncertainties of a wide-open task, or if the choices have led to an attempt for which he does not possess the skills or understanding, then the teacher can narrow down the task specification, so helping the pupils to a positive achievement, albeit in a less ambitious task. Where the teacher is responsible for the assessment for external purposes, she can make allowance for this help. Some agreed schemes for doing this are needed, although one that has been used for practical science work, which is to deduct a mark for every piece of help that is given, seems crudely inflexible.

Assessment Evidence

The foresight in designing a task, and the specification that the planning serves to formulate, should envisage the ways in which the performance and/or product is to be assessed. One source of evidence can come from observation — which has to be sharply focused on the outcome criteria if it is to be conducted 'on the hoof'. Where an end product is called for, then this, be it artefact, or an essay based on research, or an account of an investigation incorporating original results, can be 'marked'. Such a report can be given a predetermined structure. Brown and Shavelson (1996) describe alternative forms for recording results of science investigations with middle school children, which reduce the writing burden but ensure that all important details are recorded and that pupils are asked to give relevant explanations. They also explored alternative ways of scoring the outcomes. One method used an analytic approach based on detailed schedules for observation of work in progress. A second analytic method was based on a scheme for scoring the pupils' report notebooks. They also tried having teachers arrive at a holistic judgment, giving each pupil a rating on a four level scale with each level described by a fifty-word paragraph of qualitative description. There was general agreement between the results of all three, the holistic being quicker if only a summary judgment was required, but the analytic being more informative in identifying points of feedback to the pupils and to teachers. A more general account of methods of scoring, with examples of different types of analytic and holistic schemes covering a variety of types of performance, is given by Stiggins (1994, pp. 255, 271, 288), and this topic will be discussed further in the section on 'Methods' in Chapter 7.

There is often advantage in having the pupil give an oral presentation so that there can be dialogue about the constraints and the reasoning behind strategies, tactics and interpretations that may not be clear from the 'product', and in some cases the processes involved may be demonstrated. Thus this approach can tap ideas and understanding in a unique way. In developing new ways of assessing work in the arts, Ross *et al.* (1993, p. 158) found that talk was the most natural and the most productive way of evaluating pupils' creative processes and their critical appreciation of their own achievement. However, there are many difficulties. In an assessment discussion, the teacher must allow a pupil ample time to think about a question before responding, and must listen sensitively in order to pick up clues about a pupil's thinking which might need to be followed up. Where oral discussion is organized as a set part of an assessment, recording is essential, for it is not possible both to concentrate on careful management of the interaction and to evaluate and record the responses at the same time. As in other aspects of assessment, the threats of subjectivity and bias can be reduced by linking actions to clearly specified aims and criteria (Stiggins, 1994, Chapter 9).

Such careful dialogue can also help with one aspect of performance which receives too little attention: insofar as performance assessment should be formative, the scheme of assessment should be transparent to pupils and informative in respect of their learning. In this respect also, it should not be assumed that evaluation of work should lead only to numerical marks or to a letter grade. The evaluation outcome could well supplement or replace these with a profile with each component covering a separate aspect of performance. It could also be qualitative — the pupil receiving a written or oral explanation of the strengths and weaknesses of her work.

There is a long tradition of practice, but less of research, in the assessment of practical and product performances in the GCSE and A-level examinations. There has been some use of surrogates — tests on paper to serve as substitutes for expensive tests with equipment, despite the evidence that these convey little about practical capabilities. The examining groups have developed a great deal of experience in setting out schemes of guidance for assessment of normal or selected classroom work by teachers, with the associated moderation procedures. These issues will be discussed in more detail in Chapter 7.

Group Work

Classroom work often involves work in groups, and so authentic assessment requires that the group aspect of the work be explored. Where the group work is simply a means, the task is to disentangle the achievement of individuals from the group process, but where collaboration in groups is an end in itself, the contribution to the group process is an aspect to be assessed (Wood, 1991, Chapter 16).

Assigning marks on the basis of observation is difficult because the observation has to be intensive if it is to be effective for this purpose. Marking by the output products of individuals has been shown to be unsatisfactory because a pupil's report can be selective. Interviews conducted with pupils after a group task have shown that the student who really understood what the group was doing did not necessarily produce the most highly rated reports, being surpassed on this by a student who also appeared confident during the work but who turned out on interview to have relied on the thinking of others. Various techniques have been used for the group process itself. One is to mark the group as a whole and then give the members a total of marks to be divided out amongst themselves by negotiation. Another is to take the marks of the individual products, and then give every member the same mark — which might be the mean or the lowest of the set of individual marks. Stiggins (1994) gives an interesting example of a scoring scheme for assessing the quality of a group's collaboration based on the way that a group makes an oral presentation of work on a history task to their class (pp. 289–92).

Validity and Reliability drawback

The prospects for satisfactory validity seem to be assured for this type of assessment. The activities are evidently valid, but it can only follow that the assessment is valid if the schemes of marking or scoring reflect and respect this potential in the task performances. Assessors might well be distracted by the complex nature of the performances to be observed and the products to be judged, and might focus on secondary features rather than on the central aims for which the task was originally proposed. Marking schemes might fail to capture important and unusual characteristics, particularly if they are too rigidly analytic. There are also dangers of bias, which could be particularly serious given the ephemeral nature of some of the evidence, the dependence of the result on the interaction between the individual teacher and the pupil, and the small numbers of different tasks against which any one pupil might be assessed. The validity would also be in question if pupils had not been clearly briefed or if the conditions were not recorded or controlled. It might also be objected that it would be difficult to make valid inferences if pupils were trained in performance assessment work in the same way that they have always been trained for traditional forms of testing. However, if the task really is authentic then such training would be indistinguishable from good teaching and the objection fails.

Reliability may also pose serious problems. There has been research to show that adequate reliability of marking can be achieved with careful training, and with the use of more than one rater — here the general principles are similar to those discussed for essays. A different difficulty concerns the generalizability of the results. The numbers of different performance tasks that a pupil can carry out can be quite small — results have often to be based on five short experiments, or a single project. Whether or not a pupil's performance could be very different on other tasks drawn from the same assessment domain is a question that can only be answered empirically and the answer is bound to depend on the nature of the domain. Here the work of Shavelson *et al.* (1993) on assessment of science investigations is exemplary. They used several investigation tasks which were similar in structure and difficulty, but with each set in a different context. They were able to show that an adequately stable assessment of a pupil's performance would require taking an average score of at the very least three, and, to be more comfortable, about seven different investigation tasks simply because of the variation in pupils' performances between different tasks.

This example was already mentioned in passing in the discussion of the issue of reliability in relation to domain referencing in Chapter 5. The present discussion here is about the same issue, restricted to the particular domains of performance assessment. The example discussed earlier, from the APU science work and from Lehman's study of the ratings of compositions, add further to the evidence that large numbers of performance tasks may be

Something teachers do not have

needed to ensure reliability. No public examination system in the UK has explored its potential problems with domain sampling with the degree of rigour of the three research exercises quoted here.

Planning and Assembling a Test

An Expensive Example

Some of the main issues to be raised here may be illustrated by an example of a summative test used for certification of pupils. This is the examination in physics in the UK set up for the Nuffield Advanced Physics course: a high-stakes test since the result can determine one's chances of entry to tertiary education (Morland, 1994).

The examination is in six parts, A to F, which are described in *Table 2*. The marks for the last two components, E and F, are based on assessments by the candidate's own teacher. Both of them require students to think, plan, test, check, reflect and review. Teachers mark the work using criteria supplied by the examining board. Each school has to send five marked samples to the examination board so that standards of marking can be checked. If discrepancies are found, further samples may be called for and marks may be adjusted. This assemblage illustrates some of the main strategic decisions that have to be made in designing an examination and the principles which underlie these. The issues may be summarized as follows:

Table 2: *The six components of an A-level physics examination*

	Title	No. of questions or tasks	Time	Weight in marks	Description
A	Coded Answer	40	75 min.	20%	Multiple choice questions, all to be attempted.
B	Short Answer	7 or 8	90 min.	20%	Short with structured sub-components, fixed space for answer, all to be attempted.
C	Comprehension	3	150 min.	24%	a) Answer questions on a new passage. b) Analyse and draw conclusions from a set of presented data. c) Explain phenomena described in short paragraphs: select 3 from 5.
D	Practical Problems	8	90 min.	16%	Short problems with equipment set up in a laboratory: all to be attempted.
E	Investigation	One	About 2 weeks	10%	In normal school laboratory time investigate a problem of the pupil's own choice.
F	Project Essay	One	About 2 weeks	10%	In normal school time, research and write about a topic chosen by the pupil.

- The examination was designed to reflect all of the main aims of the learning: the different components listed in *Table 2* reflected the following range of aims:

  — knowledge and understanding over a broad range of topics,
  — ability to learn new physics,
  — skills in handling laboratory equipment and in data analysis,
  — ability to take initiative in practical investigations,
  — ability to research a new topic and synthesize the findings.

- The examination was designed to match the pupils' opportunities to learn: in this case, the course aims were worked through in a set of curriculum materials and the examiners' task was to be faithful to these.
- Each aim was assessed in the most appropriate and economical way: thus short answer questions served to assess ability to make simple calculations, practical skills were assessed with equipment, investigation capability could only be assessed over a long period in classroom conditions.
- The cognitive level of the questions was monitored by reviewing the overall demands of the questions in relation to broad categories of knowledge, simple understanding and so on.
- Authentic assessment tasks were incorporated, assessed by teachers, and rigorously moderated.
- A variety of types of assessment, questions and procedures and so on, was used: this reduces the threat of bias due to question type, and gives each entrant a number of different occasions and a number of different types of challenge.

All of the above help to ensure both validity and reliability. However, this examination is relatively expensive to prepare, to conduct and to mark; it has been used only with numbers of the order of 5000 to 10000 per year. More compromises would have to be made, in reducing the variety and range of the assessments, if resources were restricted and/or numbers were much larger.

It may be asked whether a less expensive system could be used using surrogate or alternative methods. Evidence that surrogate tests are invalid has already been discussed. A large scale experiment to explore an alternative to Advanced Level was carried out in the UK in the 1970s (Wood, 1991, Chapter 17). A 'Test of Academic Aptitude' (TAA) was composed using ideas and material from the USA Scholastic Aptitude Test, widely used in that country to help determine selection for higher education, and incorporating separate tests of mathematical and verbal aptitude as a model. A sample of school students was followed through their A-levels and their subsequent university courses. The correlations of A-levels with degree results have always been low, but the correlations of the TAA were even lower, leading to the conclusion that the tests were of little value in predicting degree course success. It was also found that if the results of the new test were combined with the A-level results, they added nothing of significance to the predictive value of the A-levels. In addition, the claim that these tests measure aptitude independently of the particular learning experience of those taking them was not supported — those doing courses using mathematics at A-level did better in the mathematical components, those doing humanities courses did better with the verbal components.

Choices and Alternatives

A further strategic decision in any design concerns the incorporation of candidate choice of questions in test papers. In the Nuffield Physics example above, choice is given only in the third section of component C (select three out of five), although of course there is a wide choice in components E and F. The overall evidence is that choice does not help candidates — some students examined after a test have been shown to perform better on questions that they did not choose than on those that they did (Wood, 1991, pp. 16–18). To offer choice is to add, to the abilities being tested, the ability to choose wisely. At the same time of course, offering a choice of questions makes it more difficult to secure overall validity and reliability of the test.

Where the range of candidate performances is very wide, another strategic choice arises — whether to give the same examination to all, or to set separate papers, with the easier ones giving access only to a restricted range of grades. Such tiered papers should in principle enhance the overall reliability and validity of the examination, and help ensure that candidates do not have to spend time on questions which are too hard, or too easy for them. However, there are severe problems in putting the results of separate papers onto a common single scale. Common questions can be put on different papers, but questions turn out to have different properties in different test contexts. In addition, distortions may arise because teachers and candidates may not make optimum choices of option. There is some evidence, for example, that girls may under-perform in mathematics at GCSE because they are less likely than boys to take any small risk involved in choosing the most difficult option.

Preparation, Analysis and Administration

It is notoriously difficult to predict how pupils will respond to test questions. Wherever possible, questions should be tested out with a small sample of pupils who have similar learning backgrounds. Fixed response questions are routinely pre-tested in this way, but other types might well be with advantage. The ideal sequence is to pilot with a few pupils with whom their responses can be discussed, the purpose here being to clear up misleading or ambiguous wording and unreasonable demands. Then in a second stage the questions are tried with a larger sample representing a cross-section of the target group for the completed test.

The marks obtained in such trials should be analysed statistically. The time allowance in relation to the numbers and lengths of questions can then be checked. The difficulties of the questions are scrutinized — those that are very hard or very easy being modified or rejected, and the overall distribution of marks given by those selected is examined to check that it is not too narrow or too broad. The sequence in which the questions are presented in the final format might be adjusted so that candidates are not demoralized by meeting some of the most difficult questions at the outset. The sample of pupils taking the trial can be divided into (say) three equal groups on the basis of high or low scores, and for each question the difference in success rate between the high scoring and the low scoring thirds of the pupils can be calculated. If this difference is small or negative, this indicates that the question is either testing something which the majority of the other questions do not test, or that it is flawed in other ways. It is a matter of judgment whether such a question is then rejected or modified.

The trial results can also be used to try out and modify mark schemes. Between the selection and marking processes, it is possible to adjust the overall score distribution that will be obtained. More difficult decisions arise in an examination, such as the one described above, where there are several components. The effective weight of any one component depends mainly on the distribution of its scores. For example, one of a set of papers might be accorded a high proportion of the total marks, but if it turned out that every candidate secured almost the same score on it, it would have almost no effect in determining the final rank order. Thus, in adding components, both their overall means and their spreads ought to be scrutinized. The weights and the spreads might then be adjusted, but to start doing this is to enter a technical minefield (Wood, 1991, Chapter 10).

Pre-testing is not always possible, but where questions can be collected and stored for future use, modifications suggested by their original use and/ or data obtained from that occasion can be stored with them. In this way, any teacher or school department can build up their own question bank, so that future collections can be assembled on the basis of known characteristics. This is the idea behind question banks — examination boards and other test agencies set up their own banks for this purpose, and some banks are made available for use by teachers (as in Scotland for national assessment).

Macro Systems

The most common form of large scale assessment system is the written examination taken by all pupils at the end of a school year. When the new public examinations at age 16 were being designed in the UK, the title of the operation was *A single system of examining at 16+*, making clear that a single examination paper was not necessarily the outcome. In fact the outcome contains both papers of different levels of difficulty with correspondingly restricted access to given grades, and use of teacher assessments to produce a proportion of the total marks, and oral and some practical examinations.

Graded Assessment Schemes

Two main variants on this pattern have been explored — both have in common that they attempt to collect and use assessment and test data produced at several times rather than within a single short period at the end of a school's year. The first of these is the graded assessment. This originally started in the teaching of modern languages (Harrison, 1983), the aim being to give pupils short term targets and assessed rewards, these to form part of a learning sequence so that a pupil could progress from one achievement to the next. The highest ambition was that terminal assessment would be replaced by certification based on the level of achievement that a pupil had reached at the end of the school course.

The idea was copied into several subjects by several examining boards (Pennycuick and Murphy, 1986). Each has its own particular structure. In the Graded Assessments in Science Project (GASP), to take one example, students accumulate certificates throughout the five years of compulsory secondary schooling (Swain, 1988). Each certificate represents success in a specified combination of easy, medium and hard assessments, which can be achieved within a very flexible set of requirements. Thus, *content* is assessed by drawing on a large bank of items which cover many different curricular approaches, *process skills* are to be assessed in a variety of contexts, and skill in *explorations* can likewise be covered in class work using the teachers' own selection from a range of task proposals. The requirements ensure a balance across the three dimensions of *content, process and explorations.* The use of external banks of items and the need to work to external criteria and produce samples of pupils' work to justify judgments help to ensure fairness between schools and comparability of standards with the normal terminal external examination routes.

A critical review at a stage when several of the schemes were becoming operational is given by Brown (1989). The growth of these as alternatives to courses with conventional terminal examinations was rapid at first. They required extra work from teachers, but the burdens were taken on by teachers who found that they had a marked effect on motivating pupils throughout their secondary school years. However, the procedures for monitoring the school assessments were expensive, and the movement suffered a serious setback from government decisions that teacher assessed components should be restricted and that all public examinations should include an externally set terminal examination.

Modular Assessment

The second variant is the introduction of modular assessment. Here, the conventional syllabus is replaced by a collection of modules, each designed to take on the order of a term's teaching, amongst which schools can choose, within certain restrictions. Each is assessed separately, by a supplied test taken at the end of the module or at a set examination time within the years of the study, and there may also be a teacher assessed component. A notable feature has been the opportunity to re-take any single-module examination to redeem failure. A GCSE or A-level certificate was to be awarded on the basis of passes in a prescribed number of modules — six being the most usual number. Here again, the development has been curtailed by those who regard this as a too easy alternative to the conventional terminal examination scheme. Constraints, including a requirement to add a summative terminal examination and limits on the numbers of re-takes, are being instituted.

Portfolios and Records

Portfolio assessment is another approach that falls within this category. In principle, it rests on all that has been written above, in that a portfolio is a collection of pieces of work some of which will be, or have been, used for performance assessment. However, some users include conventional tests, others will only include results from authentic tasks, and others again might include a far broader record of a pupil's work.

The UK development was given impetus in moves to develop Records of Achievement. These are meant to give a comprehensive record of all aspects of a pupil's life in school, including but going well beyond class-room learning. They were welcomed because they could help to recognize achievements of pupils whose main strengths are not academic and because they could provide employers with information, particularly about the way in which pupils contributed within a community, which they need to have and which examination certificates do not give. The profusion of approaches which developed in the 1970s and 80s was given impetus by central funding in 1984 and by the setting up of a large evaluation project. However, enthusiasm subsequently cooled, although a National Record of Achievement was launched in 1991. The development has been marked by tensions between the formative and summative philosophies. The formative emphasis implies that pupils negotiate the record and have to come to agreement as to its contents and its judgments. Some found it hard to give pupils this degree of authority. A further problem is that the records, being broad in scope, can intrude on personal rights of privacy by exposing all aspects — of a pupil's work, relationships, and beliefs — to appraisal, discussion and recording. The National Record now imposes a summative framework, thereby weakening the formative advantages (Broadfoot, 1986; 1996, pp. 191–4).

Portfolio programmes have also attracted increasing attention and investment in the US of recent years. Some initiatives have been at local school or district level, but one of the motivations has been to set up state systems based on classroom assessment, both to improve school's reports and graduation procedures for individuals and to complement or even replace the state systems, based on external standardized tests, for monitoring school performance. The key features of any such system are the criteria for the selection of pieces of work, the criteria for scoring them, the time span over which they are collected, and the extent to which there is pupil involvement in the selection, or in the assessment. A leading example has been a state-wide initiative in Vermont, which introduced portfolio assessments in writing, science and mathematics for pupils at ages 9 and 13 (grades 4 and 8). The writing portfolio was to consist of a single best piece, and a number of other pieces to meet a set of type specifications. In mathematics between five and seven best pieces were to be submitted, chosen between teachers and students. The scoring scales set out level criteria in several dimensions, such as problem solving and communication. In general, for state reporting the scoring was done by teachers who had not taught the pupils. A thorough evaluation revealed that, in spite of the extra work involved, most teachers welcomed the initiatives and saw distinct advantages in pupils' involvement and in the broadening of the scope of their work. However, it was also revealed that the reliability of the marking was low, with unsatisfactory agreement between different markers and, in mathematics, large variation in the performance of a student from one task to another. Thus, the training of the teachers in marking, and the extent of work assessed, might have to be extended, calling into question the cost (Koretz *et al.*, 1994). Other state experiments have shown better reliability, but at the expenses of using standardized tasks so inhibiting the classroom implementation.

Survey Approaches

Some of the main features of surveys have already been discussed in the section on accountability in Chapter 4 and in relation to domain referencing in Chapter 5. The outstanding feature is that they enable a large range of sets of assessment exercises to be deployed by using, for each set, only the minimum number of pupils needed for an adequate national sample. For the APU surveys in the UK, for example, a sample of about thirty pupils would be given the tests in any one school, although different pupils would attempt different tests in order to ensure that each test was distributed over a large number of schools. The design of this distribution is known as a matrix design, so that overall the approach used was described as a matrix light sampling.

The team undertaking the APU assessment in science took advantage of this approach to tackle the problem of ensuring adequate domain referencing. Their aim was to report on a number of different domains, each representing one aspect of the aims of learning in science. What had to be determined was how the mean scores over the pupil samples would vary from question to question over a domain, and hence how large the sample of questions from any one domain might have to be. The problem of sampling the domain of possible questions could be tackled by having more packages of questions, but then each would be taken by few pupils and the problem of sampling over pupils would arise. Trials had to be conducted to determine the statistical properties of the various domain tests, so that an optimum balance between these two sampling needs could be specified.

A large scale survey need not be so ambitious. The APU science exercise did aim at generalization over some domains, but for other areas this was not attempted and the emphasis was on reporting single items. APU surveys in the other subjects were less ambitious in this respect. What was more important, to all of them, was the model of learning in the subject that they adopted as the basis for their assessment framework. The reporting of results within that framework was bound to influence the adoption of that framework as a model for the subject in schools. (For problems in language see White and Gorman (1989); for science see Black (1990).)

A second enduring problem was that the results could be of little use in policy guidance unless the variations in performance could be related to such variables as teacher training, school size and resources, class size, socio-economic background of school catchments, and so on. Political difficulties made it impossible to obtain measures of some of these and when important sources of variation cannot be allowed for — the notable omission in this case being data on pupils' socio-economic background — then other smaller effects are hard to pick up. The analyses illustrated other lessons about the difficulty of interpreting score correlations. The data seemed to show, for example, that performance was better for pupils in larger classes. However, the common practice in schools was to put pupils with special learning problems in rather smaller classes than the rest and these groups were probably responsible for the observed tendency. Also, the range of class size for which adequately large samples were available was too small. In general, where test results are used for accountability purposes, there is a need to collect a large body of data about the factors thought to be associated with performance and to conduct a complex analysis to disentangle the web of relationships between performance and these various factors. To produce results against one selected variable making no allowance for any of the others is likely to mislead. The interpretation of relationships is also difficult because correlations even when properly isolated by statistical means cannot by themselves offer proof of causes (Woodhouse and Goldstein, 1996). The problems raised here have much in common with the problems of using test results for judging schools, as discussed also under accountability in Chapter 4.

Large scale surveys have been important in other countries — notably in the USA through the work of the National Assessment of Educational Progress (NAEP). This exercise has been in operation for over twenty-five years (Lapointe, 1986) and, unlike the APU which was discontinued within ten years of its foundation, is still going strong. This exercise was also based on matrix light sampling. The range of test methods used initially was, within the US testing tradition, far narrower than in the APU, but has expanded over time (Gipps, 1990). A review of the programme in 1987 expressed concern that the narrowness of the exercise would distort the work of schools (Cohen, 1990, p. 42). The range of background variables was always limited. The work started with the aim of giving only an overall national report, but the design was later modified so that reports are now given state by state (Alexander and James, 1987).

Surveys in Australia had an even shorter life span, from 1976 to 1980, than those in the UK, and covered only basic skills in reading, writing and numeracy. Another set of surveys is at present in train in New Zealand. Here, there is great stress on making the assessment as valid and as close to the authentic as possible, with extensive use of video both to present test contexts and to record some aspects of pupils' performance. The emphasis is on reporting in depth on individual and educationally compelling items (Crooks and Flockton, 1993; Flockton and Crooks, 1994), no attempt being made to have large numbers in order to make generalization possible. International surveys will be discussed briefly in Chapter 9.

Summary

- There is a wide range of methods available for assessment: the choice has to be matched to the purposes and to constraints on time and cost.
- Fixed response questions have many advantages, notably in coverage and reliability of scoring, but can have bad feedback effects on learning habits.
- Closed response questions give more information about pupils' thinking and can still take little time and use well controlled marking procedures.
- Essay questions are unique in exploring complex structures of knowledge and reasoning; the intended demands have to be specified to

pupils in some detail, and the problems of reliable marking have to be tackled, in particular by use of multiple marking of each response.

- Authentic assessments can be made of a variety of classroom tasks and automatically meet some of the requirements for validity; however, the selection of appropriate tasks, and the procedures for ensuring reliability in assessment across different teachers and tasks, both require careful attention.

- Both the reliability and validity of a test result can be enhanced if cost and time can permit the deployment of a range of methods, so that the results that they supply can be combined.

- Good quality tests can only be formulated if the questions and procedures can be refined through pilot and trial exercises.

- A variety of approaches — portfolio assessment, graded assessment, modular assessment and records of achievement — have enriched the approaches to testing by breaking away from the dominance of the single terminal test and by promoting a widening of the range of pupils' characteristics that can be assessed and attested.

Bibliography

AIRASIAN, P.W. (1991) *Classroom Assessment*, New York: McGraw Hill. Chapters 6 and 7.

CALFEE, R. and PERFUMO, P. (1996) *Writing Portfolios in the Classroom: Policy and Practice, Promise and Peril.* Mahwah NJ, Lawrence Erlbaum, Mainly on writing. See Chapters 1, 2, 10 and 15.

DARLING-HAMMOND, L., ANCESS, J. and FALK, B. (1995) *Authentic Assessment in Action Studies of Schools and Students at Work*, New York: Teachers' College Press. A study based upon detailed case-studies of innovations in teachers' assessments in five schools in or near New York. See particularly Chapters 1 and 7.

GIPPS, C.V. (1994) *Beyond Testing: Towards a Theory of Educational Assessment*, London: Falmer Press. Chapter 6.

ROSS, M., RADNOR, H., MITCHELL, S. and BIERTON, C. (1993) *Assessing Achievement in the Arts*, Buckingham: Open University Press. Particularly Chapters 3 and 5.

SALVIA, J. and HUGHES, J. (1990) *Curriculum Based Assessment: Testing What is Taught*, New York: Macmillan. Has useful general chapters, and chapters on specific areas — reading (Chapter 6), mathematics (7), written language (8), adaptive and social behaviour (9) and learning strategies (10).

STIGGINS, R.J. (1994) *Student-Centered Classroom Assessment*, New York: Merrill/Macmillan. Chapters 6 on fixed response, Chapter 7 on essays, Chapters 8 and 11 on performance assessment.

WOOD, R. (1991) *Assessment and Testing*, Cambridge, Cambridge University Press. Chapters 1 to 5, 9, 10, 13 and 15 to 19.

References

AIRASIAN, P.W. (1991) *Classroom Assessment*, New York: McGraw Hill.

ALEXANDER, L. and JAMES, H.T. (1987) *The Nation's Report Card: Improving the Assessment of Student Achievement*, Washington DC: National Academy of Education.

BARLEX, D., BLACK, P.J., HARRISON, G. and WISE, D. (1995a) *Resource Task File: Nuffield Design and Technology*, Harlow: Longman.

BARLEX, D., BLACK, P.J., HARRISON, G. and WISE, D. (1995b) *Capability Task File: Nuffield Design and Technology*, Harlow: Longman.

BAXTER, G.P. and SHAVELSON, R.J. (1994) 'Science performance assessments: Benchmarks and surrogates', *International Journal of Educational Research*, **21**, pp. 279–98.

BLACK, P.J. (1990) 'APU science — the past and the future', *School Science Review*, **72**, pp. 13–28.

BROADFOOT, P. (1986) *Profiles and Records of Achievement: A View of Issues and Practices*, London: Holt Saunders.

BROADFOOT, P. (1996) *Education, Assessment and Society*, Buckingham: Open University Press.

BROWN, M. (1989) 'Graded assessment projects: Similarities and differences', in MURPHY, P. and MOON, B. (eds) *Developments in Learning and Assessment*, London: Hodder and Stoughton, pp. 300–11.

BROWN, J.H. and SHAVELSON, R.J. (1996) *Assessing Hands-on Science: A Teacher's Guide to Performance Assessment*, California: Corwin/Sage.

BUNDERSON, C.V., INOUYE, D.K. and OLSEN, J.B. (1989) 'The four generations of computerized educational measurement', in LINN, R.L. (ed.) *Educational Measurement*, 3rd edition, New York: Macmillan, pp. 367–408.

COHEN, D. (1990) 'Reshaping the standards agenda: From an Australian's perspective of curriculum and assessment', in BROADFOOT, P., MURPHY, R. and TORRANCE, H. (eds) *Changing Educational Assessment: International Perspectives and Trends*, London: Routledge, pp. 32–51.

CROOKS, T. and FLOCKTON, L. (1993) *The Design and Implementation of National Monitoring of Educational Outcomes in New Zealand Primary Schools*, Dunedin: HEDC University of Otago.

DARLING-HAMMOND, L., ANCESS, J. and FALK, B. (1995) *Authentic Assessment in Action: Studies of Schools and Students at Work*, New York: Teachers' College Press.

FLOCKTON, L. and CROOKS, T. (1994) *Assessment Tasks for National Monitoring of Educational Outcomes in New Zealand Primary Schools*, Dunedin: HEDC University of Otago.

GAULD, C.F. (1980) 'Subject oriented test construction', *Research in Science Education*, **10**, pp. 77–82.

GIPPS, C. (1990) 'National assessment: A comparison of English and American trends', in BROADFOOT, P., MURPHY, R. and TORRANCE, H. (eds) *Changing Educational Assessment: International Perspectives and Trends*, London: Routledge, pp. 53–64.

GIPPS, C.V. (1994) *Beyond Testing: Towards a Theory of Educational Assessment*, London: Falmer Press.

HARRISON, A. (1983) *A Review of Graded Tests*, London: Methuen Educational.

HARTOG, P. and RHODES, E.C. (1936) *The Marks of Examiners*, London: Macmillan.

KORETZ, D., STECHER, B., KLEIN, S. and McCAFFREY, D. (1994) *The Vermont Portfolio Assessment Program: Findings and Implications*, Los Angeles: University of California-CRESST and Rand Institute.

LAPOINTE, A.E. (1986) 'Testing in the USA', in NUTTALL, D.L. (ed.) *Assessing Educational Achievement*, London: Falmer Press, pp. 114–24.

LINN, R.L. (ed.) (1989) *Educational Measurement*, 3rd edition, New York: Macmillan.

MILLMAN, J. and GREENE, J. (1989) 'The specification and development of tests of achievement and ability', in LINN, R.L. (ed.) *Educational Measurement*, 3rd edition, New York: Macmillan, pp. 335–66.

MORLAND, D. (1994) *Physics: Examinations and Assessment. Nuffield Advanced Science*, Harlow: Longman.

PENNYCUICK, D.B. and MURPHY, R.J.L. (1986) 'The impact of the graded test movement on classroom teaching and learning', *Studies in Educational Evaluation*, **12**, pp. 275–79.

ROSS, M., RADNOR, H., MITCHELL, S. and BIERTON, C. (1993) *Assessing Achievement in the Arts*, Buckingham: Open University Press.

SHAVELSON, R.J., BAXTER, G.P. and GAO, X. (1993) 'Sampling variability of performance assessments', *Journal of Educational Measurement*, **30**, pp. 215–32.

STIGGINS, R.J. (1994) *Student-Centred Classroom Assessment*, New York: Merrill/Macmillan.

SWAIN, J. (1988) 'GASP The graded assessments in science project', *School Science Review*, **70**, pp. 152–8.

TAMIR, P. (1990) 'Justifying the selection of answers in multiple-choice questions', *International Journal of Science Education*, **12**, pp. 563–73.

WHITE, J. and GORMAN, T. (1989) 'APU Language assessment: Some practical consequences of a functionally oriented approach', in MURPHY, P. and MOON, B. (eds) *Developments in Learning and Assessment*, London: Hodder and Stoughton, pp. 312–22.

WOOD, R. (1991) *Assessment and Testing*, Cambridge: Cambridge University Press.

WOODHOUSE, G. and GOLDSTEIN, H. (1996) 'The statistical analysis of institution-based data', in GOLDSTEIN, H. and LEWIS, T. (eds) *Assessment: Problems, Developments and Statistical Issues*, Chichester and New York: John Wiley, pp. 135–44.

Chapter 7

Teachers' Roles in Assessment and Testing

Introduction

It is clear that in formative assessment, the central role belongs to teachers. It is arguable whether or not they also have a role in assessment for certification or for accountability. At the same time the following quotation, written in 1986, underlines an important feature:

> Consider the amount of time, energy and money spent by both individual teachers, and schools in general, on setting and marking continuous assessment tests, end of session examinations and mock 'O' levels. Reflect on the money spent by examination boards and the number of assessment specialists employed by them. Read, if you can find a sabbatical term, the literature on the technology of assessment for reporting and certification. Compare these in turn with the complete lack of support normally given to teachers in devising and applying procedures to pinpoint their students' learning problems, with the virtual absence of outside agencies to develop formative assessment instruments and procedures, and the limited literature on the topic. (Black, H. 1986, p. 7)

This neglect seems all the more surprising in the light of three significant considerations. These are:

- It seems self-evident that good quality feedback is essential to effective teaching and learning.
- There is well documented research evidence that formative assessment linked to good learning practice does indeed give improved learning (Black, P.J. 1993(a), pp. 54–6; Crooks, 1988).
- Assessment by teachers can make a strong contribution to overcoming some of the serious problems of obtaining valid assessments for certification and for accountability.

The presentation in this chapter will start with a discussion of formative assessment and its close link to the improvement of learning. This will establish some principles, in the light of which the next section can review the present state of practice, taking up some of the implications of the situation described in the above quotation. This will lead naturally to a section on techniques for developing formative assessment. The discussion then turns to the role of teachers in summative and certification assessment, followed by a section on the tensions between the formative and summative roles. A final summary reviews implications for the future.

Evidence for Learning

Formative assessment requires the use of a diverse set of data for a purpose. That purpose is the modification of the learning work to adapt to the needs that are revealed by the evidence. Only when assessment evidence is acted upon in this way does it become formative. Such response to feedback may range from the immediate classroom response to a question, through to a comprehensive review of a variety of data in order to appraise progress over a whole topic or theme. In terms of control theory, the use of feedback in this way would seem to be an obvious necessity.

Assessment of a student's response to any activity involves an interpretation of that response. For example, the teacher concentrating on the formative purpose will be looking for evidence of any obstacle of misunderstanding with which the student needs help, whereas for the summative purpose, the task is to determine the extent to which the student's work has met given target criteria (Wiliam and Black, 1996).

Authentic Evidence

It follows from the findings about 'Validity and learning' discussed in Chapter 4 that the design and interpretation of assessment work has to be conducted within a strategy concerned with the development of the active and thoughtful learner. Such active learning is quite different from passive reception learning, and calls for a broader range of assessment activities. This point is illustrated by the following comment from a teacher in Spain:

> . . . this diversity of strategies for the assessment of the learning process owing to the different forms of communication that it provides for the pupils, offers the latter a greater chance of performing well in their studies. In the case of those students who have highly-developed instrumental and operative abilities or mathematical intuition, the exercises and problems based on physics and chemistry formulas enable them to demonstrate what they have learned very easily. Likewise, those students who display a more rational, divergent way of thinking, who interpret things in a more visual manner and who have powers of analysis and synthesis are able to show what they have learnt by means of . . . their activity books, reports on experiments, hypotheses based on problem solving, correlation of data and the interpretation of graphs and charts. (Black and Atkin, 1996, p. 112)

One of the tasks of the teacher is to find a language or medium in which the pupil can respond. This responsiveness is to be assured by having both diversity and flexibility in the assessment process (Darling-Hammond *et al.*, 1995, p. 258). As pointed out in the discussion of 'Authentic assessment' in Chapter 6, classroom assessment can use a far wider range of assessment evidence than is possible for external assessments, and such a range has to be used if a valid picture of a pupil's attainments and needs is to be obtained. Furthermore, in interpreting pupils' work for any of the purposes, the teacher can work in a manner different from an external examiner, as illustrated by the following extract from an account of a teacher in the Netherlands engaged in teaching a new curriculum in technology:

> The assessment of practical activities is more complicated. Most teachers also take the way in which a piece of work has been produced into account. In other words, they evaluate both the result and the way in which it was produced. The teacher's evaluation of work pieces is personal, though it has tried to use objective criteria (for example, a comparison of a drawing to guidelines in the assignment). Some teachers involve other pupils in the assessment. (Black and Atkin, 1996, p. 96)

The justification for taking into account the way in which a piece of work was produced is that any inferences drawn from the assessment result about the student's skill and understanding may be more trustworthy if this is done — thus enhancing the validity of the assessment (as defined in the quotation from Messick in Chapter 4).

The teacher's personal knowledge of the pupil, and understanding of the context of the performance, are significant advantages in securing validity in formative assessment. A further advantage arises because the closer an assessment activity can come to the actual activity to which its results are to be considered relevant, the more likely it is to satisfy validity criteria. As explained in Chapter 6, the term 'authentic assessment' serves to signify one of the strengths of classroom assessment. In striving for validity, such assessment has a better chance of success than formal timed written tests. Such formal tests are inevitably presenting a situation which is artificial and there is good evidence that such 'surrogate' forms of testing cannot serve as substitutes for authentic assessments.

Given that the purpose of formative assessment is to identify particular learning needs, it has to be criterion referenced. More precisely, it has to be domain referenced. However, the difficulties that beset domain referencing (as discussed in Chapter 4) are not so serious in the formative context, because on any one occasion only a small and well-defined element of a domain will be at issue in learning, and because there is opportunity for a diverse and flexible approach (Black and Dockrell, 1984, pp. 116–18).

The need for an approach in which activity is assessed in context is argued at a more fundamental level by Christie (1995, p. 109) in an analysis (already referred to under 'Validity and learning' in Chapter 4) of the problems of assessing the domain of reading. He proposes three potential dimensions along which a pupil's progress should be followed: maturity, skills and competencies, and contexts of performance. Any standard test designed for reliability by way of internal homogeneity is bound to focus on only one dimension, which may make the evidence useless — as Christie explains:

> . . . attempts to manipulate a predictive variable, rather than to manipulate the performance that the variable predicts, immediately destroy the set of relationships which lent the variable predictive validity in the first place. (p. 112)

To explore and work at all three requires a more flexible approach in which each piece of work is judged in terms of its particular combination of qualities in these dimensions, and guidance for a pupil would have to look at assessing and challenging progress in all three dimensions. Such an emphasis leads to the conclusion that the data that will guide in a formative way will be qualitative descriptions of the particular combination of qualities in a piece of work rather than a single number or grade.

Resources for Diagnosis

Whilst teachers' own assessments have to be closely coordinated with their teaching plans, it does not follow that external agencies have no role in supporting such work. In some countries, national assessment programmes have been based on the provision of assessment items for teachers to use as and when they find helpful — in some cases both to use the results internally and for reporting to outside agencies, so that the assessments serve both formative and summative purposes (Harlen, 1995). External provision can suggest useful frameworks for formative assessment as well as supplying test exercises for formative use. Standardized tests are unlikely to contribute because they tend to be norm-based and lacking in the detail required for useful feedback. Sets of more open questions can suffer from the same drawback of being too general, even though they may do a good job for an examiner trying to cover a field comprehensively with as few questions as possible. Where questions have been composed to serve a formative function, as in light-sampling surveys, so that the questions can cover a field more thoroughly and in detail, the resource can be of considerable value.

A national innovation in France has taken this further by setting up a requirement for national tests to be taken by all students at three stages — 3rd Grade (age 8, middle of primary school), 6th Grade (age 11, beginning of lower secondary) and 10th Grade (age 15, beginning of upper secondary). The significant feature is that these tests are taken at the beginning of a new school year, so that the emphasis is not on the past, but on diagnostic information at the outset of their school year to help the design of teaching for each class of pupils. A detailed evaluation of this initiative has been carried out for mathematics (Black and Atkin, 1996, pp. 103–8). This study revealed some important general lessons.

The innovation required the construction by experts of test items which were designed to explore critical features of students' understanding of mathematical concepts, i.e. they focused on subject competence and on cognitive development. Thus, national resources were being used to strengthen teachers' own work. This required however extensive training of the teachers, because they had to understand the strategies behind the questions in order to mark and interpret the responses in terms of critical learning needs of their students.

The information that such detailed assessment could reveal was clearly worthwhile. However, the evaluation of this innovation revealed some other important lessons about this approach to formative assessment. One was that the diagnostic information has to be up-dated frequently — as the evaluation report noted:

> While the results supply quick and useful information on a class, this information is perishable and rapidly outdated. The teachers point to not only the fleeting character of the information obtained from the results (the term 'snapshot' was more than once used) but also the deceptive picture it could give of pupils' progress even over a very short time (a few weeks). (*Ibid.*, p. 106)

More significantly, the teachers involved reported that they had considerable difficulty in making full use of the results. As one teacher expressed it:

> In our school, standards are completely uneven. You can go from the model pupil to the one who is utterly at sea. The problem for the maths teacher is to practise differential management, to navigate at several speeds . . . The gap between pupils keeps on widening whereas we should be able to narrow it. (*Ibid.*, p. 111)

The problem of providing remedial work that was suitable for this wide range of needs was very hard to solve within the established programmes and practices for classroom teaching. The evaluation report suggested that these hopes were beyond the bounds of the possible, with some teachers saying that the goal of moving from the test results to adequate remediation would be impossible to achieve.

Other important lessons illustrated by this initiative in France are taken up below.

Formative Models of Learning

Formative assessment has to be based upon a theory about the ways in which pupils learn the subject involved. In the French example, such theory was used at the outset in the formulation of the tasks to be used. The theory must be further invoked in the interpretation of any pupil's performance, for this can also require expert judgment. Here, some help may be gained from the use of general models of the development of reasoning skills. Stiggins (1994, Chapter 10) sets out accounts of the Bloom model (already mentioned in relation to analysis of cognitive demand in domain referencing in Chapter 5) and of two alternatives — suggesting that teachers should choose whichever seems more suitable for their work. It is arguable whether such general outlines can help. There may here be a difference in practice between primary teachers, who more readily think in terms of general development, and secondary teachers who focus more on the achievements specific to their subjects (Darling-Hammond *et al.*, 1995, p. 267).

The task of analysing pupils' responses in relation to some overall scheme of progress in their learning work is a demanding one. Some of the aspects involved have already been discussed in the section on 'Aggregation, profiles and progress' in Chapter 5. The work can be helped by frameworks which have been designed and refined through trial in schools. A notable example is the Primary Language record developed by the former Inner London Education Authority, and still in use in several countries (*Ibid.*, Chapter 5). This was a scheme to be used in dialogue between the child, the parents and the school, and involved a sequence of activity starting with interviews at entry to the school, first with a child's parents and then with the child. Systematic observation of the child's language use was supplemented during the year with further conferences with the family and with the child. An end-of-year summation exercise then formulated a report for the guidance of next year's teacher. The data so obtained were interpreted in terms of reading scales which could chart progress of the child from dependence to independence and from inexperience to experience in reading. Teachers using the approach reported great surprise at the relevant knowledge that parents possessed and could convey about their children's reading. A researcher summing up an evaluation of its use in a US school commented:

> It offers a holistic framework for observing and documenting the growth of children that allows for differences in teachers as well as in children. It enables teachers to understand better how children learn and thus to teach in child-centred ways. By focusing on children's strengths, by looking at them individually, by celebrating their diversity, it supports the overall quality of school instruction. (*Ibid.*, p. 195)

This seems to show that the scheme has all the essential requirements for good formative assessment, and it is unusual for any scheme to transport so successfully from one country to another. Many frameworks which set out criteria for progression can be found. Stiggins sets out several in his Chapter 11, the work by Ross *et al.* (1993) describes the development of a scheme for the arts, schemes for investigative science have been published by Brown and Shavelson (1996) and by Jones *et al.* (1992, Chapter 7). The schemes described in Chapter 6 for the graded assessment developments also have a great deal to offer. Where national or state curricula have been set out in levels of progression, as in the UK, Australia and New Zealand, these could also be useful, although, unlike most of the other examples, these have been developed by a bureaucratic process rather than by trial and modification in a range of classrooms.

The extent to which approaches can be general across different subjects has to be limited. Many believe that mathematics has to be built up hierarchically so that a topic must be mastered before moving on. In other areas, there is no such hierarchy, but rather a progress in sensitivity, in depth of critical judgment, and in power to articulate — as in study of literature or in the arts (Ross *et al.*, 1993) or in the three dimensional model of Christie for reading. Science might be different again, having well structured theoretical concepts, but also requiring a more complex and holistic approach if investigative experimental work is being pursued.

A development project for arts assessment found that the understanding of a model for the learning on the subjects was a major difficulty:

> Looking back at our early interviews with teachers, we can now redefine their problems with assessment as stemming from a fundamental difficulty as to how to reconcile the so-called 'teachable' elements of the arts curriculum with what is essentially 'untaught': conventional forms and expressive materials transmitted by subjective feelings. Having little concern for what Louis Arnaud Reid called 'embodied meaning', leaving little scope for a personal sense of form and feeling as an integrated whole — in other words with an inadequately defined knowledge base — a comprehensive, aesthetic assessment from our teachers was impossible. So they came across as uncertainly objective, apologetically subjective, and frequently as either radically blocking or simply ignoring the voice of the pupil. (*Ibid.*, p. 166)

The way of thinking revealed in this passage emphasizes the holistic, in part subjective, and context bound approach to assessment, in which it is seen as a qualitative art calling for the judgment of the connoisseur. This is worlds apart from the algorithmic, quantitative and objective paradigm that tends to persist in and through the psychometrics of testing. In part the polarization could be explained by the differences between (say) mathematics and art appreciation. However, where pupils' open-ended investigations in mathematics are to be assessed, there is pressure to move away from the algorithmic and quantitative paradigm. The emphasis by Popham on verbal description and judgment in the application of domain referencing, quoted in Chapter 4, reflects a similar shift.

Insofar as assessment can be diagnostic, the instruments ought to be fully researched and validated in relation to a learning model. Detailed exploration of pupils' progress in learning concepts shows that suitable models have to be multi-dimensional, even in the rather ascetic spheres of mathematics and science, so that here again there is no substitute for expert judgment of the particular situation of a pupil (Denvir and Brown, 1987; Simon *et al.*, 1994 and 1995; Brown *et al.*, 1995). The fact that very few small scale domains have been researched in adequate detail leads Wood (1991), in a review of this aspect of assessment, to be sceptical of any claims about diagnostic assessment, and to be critical of many schemes of progression that he sees as simplistic.

Whatever the model, it is essential to identify the student's level of conceptual comprehension and technical or methodological competence. The information collected, in homework and through feedback in class discussion, should be about *understanding* as well as about *subject knowledge* — it is more easy to ask questions and set exercises which call only for knowledge, and these, being more easy than others, may produce less trouble for all concerned. The research evidence is that where understanding is emphasized, even the recall of facts is more effective if pupils are tested more than a few weeks after the teaching (Nuthall and Alton-Lee, 1995).

Present Practice

Several common features emerge from surveys of research into formative assessment in many countries (Black, 1993(a); Black and Wiliam, 1997; Crooks, 1988). The overall picture is one of weak practice — formative assessment has a low rating in teachers' training and in their priorities. Key weaknesses are:

- Classroom evaluation practices generally encourage superficial and rote learning, concentrating on recall of isolated details, usually items of knowledge which pupils soon forget.
- Teachers do not generally review the assessment questions that they use and do not discuss them critically with peers, so there is little reflection on what is being assessed.
- The grading function is over-emphasized and the learning function under-emphasized.
- There is a tendency to use a normative rather than a criterion approach, which emphasizes competition between pupils rather than personal improvement of each. The evidence is that with such practices the effect of feedback is to teach the weaker pupils that they lack ability, so that they are de-motivated and lose confidence in their own capacity to learn.

Where extra emphasis on teacher assessment has been prescribed, as with the National Curriculum in England and Wales, the requirements have been widely misunderstood. Research evaluations have established that most teachers, particularly those in primary schools, have interpreted teacher assessment as summative assessment only. Some have collected voluminous records of pupils' work whilst having no clear strategy for using these records (McCallum *et al.*, 1993; 1995). Others have responded to calls for enhanced formative assessment by setting formal summative tests which mimic the external statutory tests. Recent surveys have also reported that there was very little formative assessment to be seen in science work (Russell *et al.*, 1995).

One outstanding reason for this weakness is that summative assessments, notably external testing, often dominate teaching because their results command greater esteem than those of other forms of assessment. Harry Black (1986, p. 9) has argued that it was the growth of external and summative examining that snuffed out the early development of formative assessment. However, there are other reasons for the weak development of the practices of formative assessment. They are to do with the many practical difficulties of collecting and recording evidence in the midst of all the other demands of everyday teaching, and with the challenges presented by the prospect of amending, or repeating, or differentiating teaching to respond to assessment evidence.

In a classroom, teachers are likely to look for feedback to confirm the success of their own performance. Their priority may be to keep the process going and the reaction of pupils is used to judge whether it is feasible to carry on. Teachers often choose a sub-group of only a few pupils, and it is their reactions and responses to questions which serve to justify proceeding. In an atmosphere where a fast pace is judged to be necessary, and particularly where a teacher is insecure, such practices serve the teachers' own purposes (Airasian, 1991, Chapter 4). The 'data' so collected may say little about the real learning of pupils. The same is often true of the practices used in setting and marking homework and written work in the classroom — an average mark of seven out of ten will be regarded as a satisfactory basis for carrying on even though it may mean, insofar as it conveys any clear meaning, that a significant fraction of the class may have grasped less than half of what was being taught.

Introduction of formative assessment in a thorough going way with a group of teachers calls for changes in their practice which are radical in scope and nature. Accounts of such changes have been produced, in work with groups of teachers in Australia (Torrie, 1989; Butler, 1995), and in England (Fairbrother, 1995). Some idea of the scope of the changes that might be entailed is illustrated by Torrie's study (1989) of work with Australian teachers and by study of the changes made in Queensland (Butler, 1995). In this latter innovation, the state abolished external tests and moved to sole reliance on school-based certification. This had little effect at first on class-room practice and it required further state initiatives to move practice away from reliance on stereotyped terminal tests towards a criterion referenced basis. This latter shift was linked to assumption by teachers of enhanced responsibility for generating their own science curricula within very broad state guidelines.

Formative assessment can be hampered by misunderstandings amongst teachers. In the UK, teachers were not clear about the purpose of the teacher assessment component of the new national assessments introduced after 1988: the natural tendency was to see teacher assessment as an exercise in predicting an examination result. Given this view, the best data that teachers could collect were the results of similar tests. The use of these to generate the results throws away all the potential strengths of teacher assessment which inhere in its being based on evidence very different from that which formal testing can elicit.

Methods

Collecting Information

Most teachers have always used a variety of sources in an informal way — it is essential to sharpen this practice with a view to eliciting more usable data. Written work by pupils, both as homework or as classroom work, can only be useful if it is both designed to reveal particular features of import-ance, evaluated with those features in mind, and marked in such a way as to convey formative messages to the pupil.

More tightly structured information can be useful. For example, a work-sheet to be completed by each student can help if the responses evoked are distinctive in that they produce detailed information in relation to statements about specific aims — i.e. they are grounded in the criterion referencing that formative assessment inevitably needs (Parkin and Richards, 1995). Such written evidence, if produced in a systematic way can relieve the teacher from the pressure of noting and recording entirely from the ephemeral evidence of classroom events. Ephemeral evidence can however have its own unique value: some teachers have found it surprisingly useful if they suspend their active teaching interventions for a time — making clear to a class what they are doing and why — and concentrate only on looking and listening with a few students at a time whilst the rest are engaged in indi-vidual or small-group activities (Cavendish *et al.*, 1990; Connor, 1990). It has also been found that teachers' learn more from looking at a few pupils in detail than in attempting to strike a common level for all — although the few have to be carefully chosen with the choice changed on each occasion (Darling-Hammond *et al.*, 1995, p. 254). There is general agreement that observing and recording observations cannot be valuable unless significant periods of time are reserved for the purpose.

The feedback obtained in dialogue can clearly be important — but its value depends on the quality of the questioning and on the care with which responses are treated. Whereas a closed question merely leaves a pupil calculating whether to take the risk on her chances of knowing the right answer, an open one can encourage self-expression and, if responses are continually treated with care, can show the pupils that the teacher is interested in their ideas. The aim should be to establish forms of classroom discourse which encourage pupils to speak honestly, where they express their thought processes knowing that these will be taken seriously and challenged to develop their thinking. Such discussion has to be so conducted that all of a class and not just a few are taking part — techniques such as organized debates, pre-specified reporting tasks on a rota, and group discussions followed by reports can all help here (Edwards and Mercer, 1989; Stiggins, 1994, Chapter 9).

Marking

For formative purposes, it will often be particular strengths or weaknesses that might be selected for feedback discussion, even though for summative purposes, an overall holistic judgment might be appropriate, if only because each analysed atomistic component cannot be judged outside the whole context in which it functions. Where the learning work is a production task rather than a responsive task — be it an investigative or a constructive project, or an essay based on library research, or an imaginative work, the choice between holistic and analytic approaches will arise. The report by Brown and Shavelson (1996) includes a discussion of three different ways of scoring the performance on open-ended science tasks — two being analytic and the third holistic. The work by Ross and colleagues on assessment in the arts leans heavily towards the holistic approach. However the two approaches are used, it seems clear that clear qualitative descriptions of the key characteristics of a piece of work are essential for both purposes, whereas marks or grades will convey little unless, in summative use, they represent stages on a sequence of generally agreed qualitative descriptions. This atomistic–holistic debate also bears upon the validity of pupils' performances. It is well established that a pupil's performance on a test of a specific skill will not serve as a guide to the capacity to select and deploy that skill in the context of a realistically complex task. Thus atomized, out-of-context assessment is of only limited value (Black, 1990).

The collection of samples of pupils' work in portfolios may also be a helpful approach, although these are more relevant to summative use, the formative aspect residing in the immediate appraisal of the individual pieces of work as they are produced, in the work of selecting pieces of work to present in a portfolio and in the preparation of a summary introduction to the portfolio, where those are undertaken in negotiation between teacher and pupil.

A particular feature of the ILEA language record, described earlier in this chapter, deserves attention at this point. Emphasis is placed on assessment of a pupil's attainment at the outset of schooling, which recognizes that pupils do not at any stage, even when first entering school, come to a learning programme without a personal portfolio of strengths and weaknesses, insights and blind spots, that will affect the new learning. The mathematics assessment in France described above also addressed this problem. Some such assessment appraisal on entry would seem to be an essential feature of any formative assessment programme wherever the quality and uniformity of assessments of previous work cannot be guaranteed. Airasian's (1991) book pays particular attention to this feature (Chapter 2).

Those who have carried out development work with schools focused on improving classroom assessment invariably lay stress on the power of collaborative work between teachers. For example, the summary of a set of such case studies in US schools (Darling-Hammond *et al.*, 1995, p. 253) emphasizes that through such discussions, based on sharing ideas in their reviews of the evidence of pupils' work, teachers can build up a mutual expertise that no-one else possesses and that no-one from outside could give them. This is described as the creation of communities of practice, and it highlights the centrality of assessment discussions in the professional development of teachers.

Bias

One important danger in formative — or summative — assessment by teachers is the threat of bias. Research in this area is reviewed in Wood's book and a full discussion has been given here in Chapter 4. There are conflicting results on whether teachers confuse or conflate industry and effort with achievement. There is evidence of teachers behaving differently towards boys and girls, towards pupils from different social classes, and towards good-looking and plain-looking pupils. In each of these cases, some teachers would rate a particular piece of work more highly if it came from one type of pupil rather than the other. There is also concern over some evidence that teachers assessments tend to be influenced by opinions about a pupil's 'ability' rather than strictly on achievement — it being suggested that teachers will tend to explain the differential responses of pupils to their efforts to teach as inevitable consequences of a predetermined 'ability'.

Acting on the Evidence

All collection of formative evidence must be guided by a strategy for ensuing action. The distinctive feature of formative assessment is that the information is used to modify the learning programme in order to make it more effective — there is little point in gathering information unless it can be acted upon. Since assessment information is sure to reveal heterogeneity in learning needs, the action has to include some form of differentiated teaching. One reason why this path is not followed was suggested by Perrenoud (1991) 'There is a desire *in everyone not to know about things about which one can do nothing*' (p. 89 author's emphasis).

The action which should follow any assessment revealing shortcomings in knowledge or understanding might have to be repetition — of the same work or of other work with the same aim — in order to ensure mastery before proceeding. This may be seen as essential in a hierarchical subject, but over-rigid and impracticable in other areas. A whole set of initiatives calling for quite radically new forms of classroom teaching was developed in the USA under the banner of mastery learning, a system in which each pupil would only move from one issue to the next when he had shown mastery of it, and would be required to repeat work after failures until success had been achieved. Significant gains have been reported, but the movement did not take a firm hold (Block *et al.*, 1989). Work in Scotland to establish formative and criterion-referenced assessment reported radical changes in the teachers' perceptions of their pupils and was seen by the authors as adapting elements of the mastery learning concept to the environment of classrooms in Scotland (Black and Dockrell, 1984, p. 56).

It is hardly possible to implant formative assessment into an existing teaching programme without changing that programme. New assessment cannot just be attached to an existing teaching scheme, it has to be built into a revision of the scheme, if only because its use to guide pupils' learning according to their different needs can only happen if the teaching plans allow the extensive time for planning and organization that such use requires: opportunities have to be created for making use of the feedback information provided by the assessment.

One approach uses large scale adaptations by placing pupils in separate streams, or sets, or tracks, but these do not deal with immediate needs. Some teachers have responded by organizing units of work into a core and extension, with the extension work varying widely, from advanced new topics for high attainers, to repetition of the basics for those in serious need (Black, 1995, p. 139). Others indicate less formal and more flexible approaches, building in revision or revisiting a problem through opportunities in later work for those in need. Affecting this last issue is the extent to which teaching programmes are flexible rather than rigid.

Effective use of assessment feedback requires teacher judgment, and the confidence and flexibility in management of a curriculum plan that can only come from ownership of such a plan. Thus it seems that, ideally, any scheme for incorporating good formative opportunities has to be constructed by teachers for themselves. In such construction, teachers' have to handle two innovations — the need to implement new methods for differentiation and flexibility in learning and the need to learn, perhaps invent, a new technology for producing the appropriate evidence of pupils' achievements.

The use of formative assessment feedback may be on an individual basis or at a more general level. Given that there is evidence that cooperative learning in groups can help motivation, inter-personal skills and learning, feedback which evaluates the work of a group overall can be used — and there is evidence that this can be effective if it is also combined with some evaluation of particular individual difficulties (Crooks, 1988).

Summative Assessment by Teachers

Collection and Selection

Some of the issues here have already been explored in Chapter 3, both in the section on 'Certification, progress and transfer' and particularly in the last section on 'Interaction of purposes'. Formative and summative functions can be regarded as two ends of a spectrum. At the formative end, the teacher conducts the assessment, makes the inferences, plans any action and will see and have to deal with the consequences, which should be short-term. At the summative end, the conduct of the assessment, drawing of inferences and the planning of action go beyond the teacher and perhaps the school. The teacher may have the whole, a part, or none of the responsibility and the consequences will arise in the medium to long term future. An end-of-year test conducted in a secondary school by a group of teachers and used both as input to reports to parents and as a basis for assignment to teaching groups in the next school year clearly lies between these extremes.

Many assessments carried out by teachers are in fact summative simply because they are not used to guide immediate changes in the teaching and learning work. This can be true even in relation to frequent homework and weekly tests, where, in the absence of effective feedback, the practice can be described as frequent summative. There can be no clear rule as to whether given assessment exercises are in themselves formative or summative — it will depend on how they relate to the pupils' work and to the way the results are interpreted and used. Some may be more useful for one purpose than the other, some may be useful for both.

A clearer grasp of the issues here can only be reached by exploring the purposes for which a teacher may need to produce summative assessments. Three possibilities can illustrate this point:

- If the purpose is as an overall guide for anyone in charge of subsequent study within the same general programme — for example,
moving from year 8 to year 9 in the same subject department —
then a profile of performance, showing strengths and weaknesses in
relation to significant criteria in the subject department's common
programme of work, would be appropriate. The information might
best be detailed, linked to the latest achievement of a pupil in each
of the areas concerned rather than to an average over time, and this
would call for little or no aggregation over components.
- If the purpose is an overall guide for a new level of study in the
same subject — for example, moving from a secondary school to a
sixth-form college to start A-level work, then a profile of a few components (as in the attainment targets of the National Curriculum)
and a summation over the last year of work might be the best guide
to potential for further study in the subject.
- If the purpose is a general guide to study in a quite new field, or
for employment where no specific component of the learning is
directly relevant, then a summation over all components and over
the last year might be best.

Any of these proposals could be implemented by using all of, a selection of, or none of the evidence gained in formative assessment work, and
this source could be supplemented or replaced by results of summative tests
set by the teacher. The process of selection and aggregation of the formative
results would be a reinterpretation in relation to the intended purpose.
Aggregation can present particular difficulties. It might seem easy to add numbers, but if these are not on a common scale the result will be meaningless.
Aggregation can only be sensible in terms of a qualitative descriptive scale to
which the component parts contribute in ways that are clearly documented.

Given that for summative results, with their medium to long term effects, mistakes are harder to rectify, the reliability of teachers' summative
assessment must be questioned. A survey of the relevant research literature
shows that assessment by teachers can attain reliabilities comparable with
those of external testing, although there are large differences between teachers
in this respect (Black, 1993(a), pp. 53–6). For example, with US science
teachers assessing for the first time open-ended practical investigations, a
programme of careful training led to their achieving a satisfactory level of
reliability (Baxter and Shavelson, 1994).

Moderation and Reliability

The reliability of teachers' assessment may be inadequate because of internal
errors in their procedures, or because of inconsistency in criteria and standards

between different teachers. Special methods for moderation are needed to achieve and ensure consistency between different teachers, both in the use of criteria and in the application of standards. One method is by teacher meetings, where a group, either within a school or between schools, exchange samples of pupils' work and discuss their assessments in relation to these. Such meetings have been found to be very valuable for the development of the teachers involved, often revealing how isolated teachers have been in respect of their standards and expectations. The points made in the previous section on 'communities of practice' are relevant here.

However, this process is expensive in requiring the meeting time of teachers, careful preparation and skilled leadership. Visit by inspectors, who can examine any practical or art-work and talk with both pupils and their teachers, are a useful alternative, although less flexible because the inspectors are constrained to be consistent across all visits, so that they cannot adjust as they learn from successive inspections. A third, and least expensive, method uses a common written test to determine a mean and spread for each teaching group, which is then used to scale the teacher's results for that group. This is economical, but involves the assumption that the group's attainment on the test will be a valid indicator of their attainment on the teacher assessed work.

All of these methods have been subject to research scrutiny in studies in the UK (Gipps, 1994, Chapter 4). The development of moderation methods was strongly supported in the growth of the Certificate of Secondary Education in the 1960s and 1970s, and went further with the preparatory studies for the establishing of the GCSE by 1988. A new slant was given by the growth of the several Graded Assessment schemes and Modular Schemes as described in Chapter 6. More recently, there have been enforced restrictions on this growth. The history of the use of moderation methods in the national assessments at ages 7, 11 and 14 is a complex and rather turbulent story which has been fully chronicled by several authors (James, 1994; Gipps, 1994, Chapters 6 and 7; Daugherty, 1995). In the broader context of 'quality assurance' for assessment results, it can be seen that many countries struggle with similar problems (Broadfoot, 1994). These vagaries raise the question of whether there are fundamental reasons why teacher assessment cannot serve a summative purpose. Harry Black (1994) describes how assessment in further education in Scotland has been a working success. The quality assurance mechanisms put in place using general descriptors as documented guides to standards, internal assurance procedures, and audit by external examiners, have established a common set of standards across the colleges, even though many of the those colleges involved have suspicions that uniformity is far from being achieved. The history of the assessment and curriculum development in Queensland is also a story of success — achieved after a long process of teachers' professional development (Butler, 1995).

Two Roles in Tension?

Insofar as teachers have to be involved in both formative and summative assessment, they are bound to experience some tension between their two roles. The former is private, focused on the learning needs of their pupils, which it must be their first concern to serve. The other has to reckon with pressures and constraints that come from outside. National and regional high-stakes systems create pressures for teachers to work within a framework which drives both their school policies and parental expectations, and the personal concern for the best interests of their pupils might have to take second place. The teacher has to hold the boundary between the different requirements of the two roles.

There is ample evidence of confusion arising from the overlap between these two roles. Attempts to enhance teacher assessment can too easily reduce in practice to greater use of that assessment for summative purposes, and to more frequent application of teacher assessments, with collection and storage of the results becoming a burden. The summative purpose requires the cumulative addition of results over time, leading teachers to concentrate on merely recording the results — each as a final outcome, and leading pupils to believe that the only purpose of assessment of performance is to add to a final score. Teachers can be tempted to formalize their assessment work so that they isolate it from learning development — indeed some think of assessment only in terms of use of standardized tests (Black, 1993(a), p. 52). Studies of assessment practices adopted by primary teachers in Britain following the introduction of the national curriculum and assessments gave evidence of all of these difficulties. Told that they were expected to produce teacher assessments, many responded by setting summative and terminal tests which were their imitation of the national assessment tests (McCallum *et al.*, 1993).

The traditional dominance of the summative function means that formative assessment struggles for its status and development. The summative function can inhibit the growth of the formative function because external tests are accepted as the model for teachers' assessments so driving these towards techniques appropriate only for summative use. External tests are a poor model for formative assessment because:

- In summative testing the need for a single overall result means that quite disparate data (for example, for practical and for theory) have to be added in ways that are often arbitrary: formative assessment does not have to do this.
- Summative assessment has peculiar problems with criterion referencing, partly because of the need to aggregate, partly because it cannot rely on personal judgments in deciding about the application of broad criteria to the work of individual pupils; such problems are far less serious in the practice of formative assessment.

- Summative work has to insist on standards of uniformity and reliability in collection and recording of data which are not needed in formative work and which inhibit the freedom and attention to individual needs that formative work requires.
- Whilst summative processes have to be seen to be 'fair' in treating all pupils in the same way, formative practice, with its priorities of identifying and helping to meet the learning needs of each pupil, can treat different pupils very differently.
- Summative tests are designed to give an overall score, so they work at low resolution and may yield little of the meaningful detail that formative feedback requires.
- Summative purposes can demand documented evidence for results — for example, for any auditing review — and so add to workload and distort formative practice, whereas formative work calls for action on the data rather than storage of it.

One way out of the dilemmas thus posed is to separate the two functions entirely, and some have recommended this, both on theoretical grounds that separate purposes require separate instruments and procedures, and on the grounds of the dilemmas for the teacher in being both friend and judge of the pupil (Harlen *et al.*, 1993; Black, 1993b).

The arguments could be separated into two components. The first is about the relation between the formative and summative roles that any teacher must adopt because the school itself has to generate summative results for its own internal purposes. Here it seems unrealistic to think, in the light of the discussion above about the range of summative assessments that teachers must make, that they can avoid all responsibility for summative work and the discussion has to be about how best to interrelate the generation and interpretation of data for the two roles, whilst keeping their separate purposes distinct. A key feature here is that it is the interpretation of the data, rather than the data as such, which might distinguish formative from summative practice (Wiliam and Black, 1996).

The second argument is about the tension between the roles within school and possible roles for public certification and accountability. Here, a separation might be attractive but has the following disadvantages:

- Some of the most important aims of education cannot be reflected in, and so supported by, assessment systems which rely only on short external testing.

Examples are practical work in science and technology, project work involving literature research or collection of data in the local community or environment, and performance in the arts. Teacher assessed summative components are essential to securing adequate validity in respect of these aspects. These necessities are recognized in the national assessments, and in all the public certificate examinations in the UK. However, to use teacher assessment for these components only tends to lower their status, the implication being that teacher assessment is a second best which is only adopted where there is no better alternative.

- External tests which are economical are bound to take only a short time.

Therefore their reliability and validity are bound to be severely constrained: they can only use a limited range of methods, and must be limited in respect of their sampling of the relevant domains. It is at least arguable that both the reliability and validity in all areas to be assessed could be enhanced by a combination of teachers' assessments and external tests.

- The status of teachers is lowered if they play no part in high-stakes testing.

As long as external tests stand for the most important functions — the high stakes of certification and accountability — teachers' assessments, both formative and summative, will be overshadowed and will not receive the priority and status that they need if they are to make their full contribution to improving learning.

None of this is to argue that the two functions are the same, nor to argue that in being responsible for both, teachers do not have to distinguish carefully between them. However, a workable relationship demands more than skill and goodwill on the part of teachers — it will also be critically dependent on the context of public policy in which they have to operate. This issue will be taken further in the discussion of systemic perspectives in Chapter 9.

Developing Good Practice

The overall weight of research evidence is that formative assessment by teachers can raise standards of learning and can improve motivation provided that it meets certain conditions (Crooks, 1988). It has to be criterion referenced rather than normative, and it must be tuned to the needs of each pupil. Blame should not be used, and praise seems to be most helpful when it is used sparingly and linked with objective advice about specific performance. The feedback has to concentrate on the most important learning goals, it has to be related to a clear model of learning progress in the subject, and it has to set high but attainable targets.

Surveys of the practice of formative assessment in several countries show that its potential to improve teaching and learning has not been exploited. Thus, this field of assessment offers distinct possibilities for the improvement of the standards of learning. However, these cannot be realized by change of assessment alone. The changes have to be part of a coherent programme in which curriculum and pedagogy are also restructured, and the tensions with summative and high-stakes factors have to be anticipated and minimized.

Overall, such visions point to a very demanding programme of development. Formative feedback implies more than correction of errors. It really needs understanding of their causes, which would tax the best learning experts. Furthermore, the student's main resource in self-adjustment is the model provided by the teacher. Students must get into the frame of reference of the teacher, to share the model of learning which gives meaning to the criteria that are reflected in assessment. Thus the development of formative assessment implies changes in role for both teachers and students (Perrenoud, 1991; Bonniol, 1991). For this reason, the discussion is incomplete without consideration of the pupils' role in assessment, which is the focus of Chapter 8.

Summary

- Formative assessment is an essential part of effective teaching and learning.
- The validity of formative assessments depends on the validity of the models of learning on which they are based.
- Current practice in formative assessment suffers from many weaknesses which might only be overcome by sustained programmes of professional development.
- Teachers can collect a wide variety of types of evidence, but these must be designed and assessed in relation to learning purposes, and with care to avoid bias.
- Teachers have also to produce summative assessments for a range of purposes, and the quality of this work and its comparability across schools can both be improved by various methods of moderation, particularly peer-group moderation.
- Summative assessment requirements readily dominate formative work because of external pressures, and will then impoverish it because formative practices provide poor models for formative work.

Bibliography

AIRASIAN, P.W. (1991) *Classroom Assessment*, New York: McGraw Hill. Chapters 2, 3, 4, 8 and 10 are all relevant.

BAIRD, J.R. and NORTHFIELD, J.R. (eds) (1992) *Learning from the PEEL Experience*, Melbourne: Monash University.

BLACK, H.D. and DOCKRELL, W.B. (1984) *Criterion Referenced Assessment in the Classroom*, Edinburgh: Scottish Council for Research in Education.

BLACK, P.J. (1993) 'Formative and summative assessment by teachers', *Studies in Science Education*, **21**, pp. 49–97.

CROOKS, T.J. (1988) 'The impact of classroom evaluation practices on students', *Review of Educational Research*, **58**, 4, pp. 438–81.

DARLING-HAMMOND, L., ANCESS, J. and FALK, B. (1995) *Authentic Assessment in Action Studies of Schools and Students at Work*, New York: Teachers' College Press. A study based upon detailed case-studies of innovations in teachers' assessments in five schools in or near New York.

FAIRBROTHER, R., BLACK, P.J. and GILL, P. (eds) (1995) *Teachers Assessing Pupils: Lessons from Science Classrooms*, Hatfield UK: Association for Science Education.

GIPPS, C.V. (1994) *Beyond Testing: Towards a Theory of Educational Assessment*, London: Falmer Press, Chapters 4, 6 and 7.

GIPPS, C. and STOBART, G. (1993) *Assessment. A Teachers' Guide to the Issues*, London: Hodder and Stoughton. Chapter 6.

PATTENDEN, J. (1995) 'Coping with assessment: An approach to recent developments (11–16)', in MARUM, E. (ed.) *Towards 2000: The Future of Childhood, Literacy and Schooling*, London: Falmer Press, pp. 148–87. Covers assessment of English, with analysis of changes since 1988, advice for departmental policies including useful samples of departmental policy and pupil assessment documents.

ROSS, M., RADNOR, H., MITCHELL, S. and BIERTON, C. (1993) *Assessing Achievement in the Arts*, Buckingham: Open University Press.

STIGGINS, R.J. (1994) *Student-Centered Classroom Assessment*, New York: Merrill/ Macmillan. Chapters 10 to 15 inclusive.

TORRANCE, H. (ed.) (1995) *Evaluating Authentic Assessment*, Buckingham: Open University Press. All chapters are relevant.

WOOD, R. (1991) *Assessment and Testing*, Cambridge: Cambridge University Press. Chapters 6 and 8.

References

AIRASIAN, P.W. (1991) *Classroom Assessment*, New York: McGraw Hill.

BAXTER, G.P. and SHAVELSON, R.J. (1994) 'Science performance assessment results: Benchmarks and surrogates', *International Journal of Educational Research*, **21**, 3, pp. 279–98.

BLACK, H. (1986) 'Assessment for learning', in NUTTALL, D.L. (ed.) *Assessing Educational Achievement*, London: Falmer Press, pp. 7–18.

BLACK, H. (1994) 'The quality of assessment in further education in Scotland', in HARLEN, W. (ed.) *Enhancing Quality in Assessment*, London: Paul Chapman, pp. 87–99.

BLACK, H.D. and DOCKRELL, W.B. (1984) *Criterion Referenced Assessment in the Classroom*, Edinburgh: Scottish Council for Research in Education.

BLACK, P.J. (1990) 'APU science — the past and the future', *School Science Review*, **72**, 258, pp. 13–28.

BLACK, P.J. (1993(a)) 'Formative and summative assessment by teachers', *Studies in Science Education*, **21**, pp. 49–97.

BLACK, P.J. (1993(b)) 'Assessment policy and public confidence: Comments on the BERA Policy Task Group's article "Assessment and the Improvement of Education"', *The Curriculum Journal*, **4**, 3, pp. 421–27.

BLACK, P. (1995) 'Lessons in evolving good practice', in FAIRBROTHER, R., BLACK, P. and GILL, P. (eds) *Teachers Assessing Pupils: Lessons from Science Classrooms*, Hatfield: Association for Science Education, pp. 137–43.

BLACK, P. and ATKIN, J.M. (1996) *Changing the Subject: Innovations in Science, Mathematics and Technology Education*, London: Routledge for OECD.

BLACK, P. and WILIAM, D. (1997) 'Assessment and Classroom Learning', *Assessment in Education* (in press).

BLOCK, J.H., EFTHIN, H.E. and BURNS, R.B. (1989) *Building Effective Mastery Learning in Schools*, New York: Longman.

BONNIOL, J.J. (1991) 'The mechanisms regulating the learning process of pupils: Contribution to a theory of formative assessment', in WESTON, P. (ed.) *Assessment of Pupils' Achievement: Motivation and School Success*, Amsterdam: Swets and Zeitlinger, pp. 119–37.

BROADFOOT, P. (1994) 'Approaches to quality assurance and control in six countries', in HARLEN, W. (ed.) *Enhancing Quality in Assessment*, London: Paul Chapman, pp. 26–52.

BROWN, M.L., BLACK, P.J., BLONDEL, E. and SIMON, S.A. (1995) 'Progression in measuring', *Research Papers in Education*, **10**, 2, pp. 143–70 and 177–79.

BROWN, J.H. and SHAVELSON, R.J. (1996) *Assessing Hands-on Science: A Teacher's Guide to Performance Assessment*, California: Corwin/Sage.

BUTLER, J. (1995) 'Teachers judging standards in senior science subjects: Fifteen years of the Queensland experiment', *Studies in Science Education*, **26**, pp. 135–57.

CAVENDISH, S., GALTON, M., HARGREAVES, L. and HARLEN, W. (1990) *Observing Activities*, London: Paul Chapman.

CHRISTIE, T. (1995) 'Defining the reading domain', in OWEN, P. and PUMFREY, P. (eds) *Children Learning to Read. International Concerns, Volume 2: Curriculum and Assessment Issues: Messages for Teachers*, London: Falmer Press, pp. 107–20.

CONNOR, C. (1990) 'National Curriculum assessment and the primary school: Reactions and illustrations of emerging practice', *The Curriculum Journal*, **1**, 2, pp. 139–54.

CROOKS, T.J. (1988) 'The impact of classroom evaluation practices on students', *Review of Educational Research*, **58**, 4, pp. 438–81.

DARLING-HAMMOND, L., ANCESS, J. and FALK, B. (1995) *Authentic Assessment in Action: Studies of Schools and Students at Work*, New York: Teachers' College Press.

DAUGHERTY, R. (1995) *National Curriculum Assessment. A Review of Policy 1987–94*, London: Falmer Press.

DENVIR, B. and BROWN, M. (1987) 'The feasibility of class administered diagnostic assessment in primary mathematics', *Educational Research*, **29**, pp. 95–107.

EDWARDS, D. and MERCER, N. (1989) *Common Knowledge*, London: Routledge.

FAIRBROTHER, R., BLACK, P. and GILL, P. (eds) (1995) *Teachers Assessing Pupils: Lessons from Science Classrooms*, Hatfield: Association for Science Education.

GIPPS, C.V. (1994) *Beyond Testing: Towards a Theory of Educational Assessment*, London: Falmer Press.

HARLEN, W. (ed.) (1994) *Enhancing Quality in Assessment*, London: Paul Chapman.

HARLEN, W. (1995) 'Standards and science education in Scottish schools', *Studies in Science Education*, **26**, pp. 107–34.

HARLEN, W., GIPPS, C.V., BROADFOOT, P. and NUTTALL, D. (1993) 'Assessment and the improvement of education, *The Curriculum Journal*, **3**, 3, pp. 215–30.

JAMES, M. (1994) 'The experience of quality assurance at Key Stage 1', in HARLEN, W. (ed.) *Enhancing Quality in Assessment*, London: Paul Chapman, pp. 116–38.

JONES, A.T., SIMON, S.A., BLACK, P.J., FAIRBROTHER, R.W. and WATSON, J.R. (1992) *Open Work in Science: Development of Investigations in Schools*, Hatfield: Association for Science Education.

McCALLUM, B., McALISTER, S., BROWN, M. and GIPPS, C. (1993) 'Teacher assessment at Key Stage 1', *Research Papers in Education*, **8**, pp. 305–27.

McCALLUM, B., McALISTER, S., BROWN, M. and GIPPS, C. (1995) *Intuition or Evidence? Teachers and National Assessment of 7-year-olds*, Buckingham: Open University Press.

NUTHALL, G. and ALTON-LEE, A. (1995) 'Assessing classroom learning: How students use their knowledge and experience to answer classroom achievement test questions in science and social studies', *American Educational Research Journal*, **32**, 1, pp. 185–223.

PARKIN, C. and RICHARDS, N. (1995) 'Introducing formative assessment at KS2: An attempt using pupil self-assessment', FAIRBROTHER, R., BLACK, P. and GILL, P. (eds) (1995) *Teachers Assessing Pupils: Lessons from Science Classrooms*, Hatfield: Association for Science Education, pp. 13–28.

PERRENOUD, P. (1991) 'Towards a pragmatic approach to formative evaluation', in WESTON, P. (ed.) *Assessment of Pupils' Achievement: Motivation and School Success*, Amsterdam: Swets and Zeitlinger, pp. 79–101.

ROSS, M., RADNOR, H., MITCHELL, S. and BIERTON, C. (1993) *Assessing Achievement in the Arts*, Buckingham: Open University Press.

RUSSELL, T., QUALTER, A. and McGUIGAN, L. (1995) 'Reflections on the implementation of National Curriculum Science Policy for the 5–14 age range: Findings and interpretation from a national evaluation study in England', *International Journal of Science Education*, **17**, 4, pp. 481–92.

SIMON, S., BLACK, P.J., BROWN, M. and BLONDEL, E. (1994) 'Progression in understanding the equilibrium of forces', *Research Papers in Education*, **9**, 2, pp. 249–80.

SIMON, S., BLACK, P.J., BROWN, M. and BLONDEL, E. (1995) *Forces in Balance*, Hatfield: Association for Science Education.

STIGGINS, R.J. (1994) *Student-Centred Classroom Assessment*, New York: Merrill/Macmillan.

TORRIE, I. (1989) 'Developing achievement based assessment using grade related criteria', *Research in Science Education*, **19**, pp. 286–90.

WILIAM, D. and BLACK, P. (1996) 'Meanings and consequences: A basis for distinguishing formative and summative functions of assessment', *British Educational Research Journal*, **22**, 5, pp. 537–48.

WOOD, R. (1991) *Assessment and Testing*, Cambridge: Cambridge University Press, Chapter 8.

Chapter 8

Pupils and Assessment

Do Pupils Have a Role?

There are both practical and fundamental reasons why pupils should play a role in their own assessment. On the practical level, if pupils' involvement means that they do some of the work for themselves, this can make it more feasible for teachers to carry through a programme of formative assessment. However, this involvement also changes both the role of the pupil as learner and the nature of the relationship between teacher and pupil, making the latter shoulder more of the responsibility for learning. This leads into the fundamental reasons why pupils involvement is essential.

This chapter starts with two stories which illustrate important issues. These lead to a discussion of pupils' expectations of assessment and testing, and so to a central question as to whether pupils can assess their own work effectively. The links between self-assessment, current insights into improved learning, and pupils' motivation and self-esteem, are then explored, leading finally to a conclusion that this is an area ripe for development.

Some Exemplary Stories

Two specific examples, each about the development of practice in a school in England, will serve to illustrate some of the issues. In the first school the science teachers wanted to use pupils' self assessment and subsequent teacher/pupil discussion as the basis for their assessments (Parkin and Richards, 1995). For each module of the course, target criteria were expressed in language accessible to pupils. For each lesson, every pupil had a sheet setting out the criteria with a space opposite each in which the pupil had to state whether the criterion was clear and had been achieved. Pupils were also asked to write in other comments — for example about enjoyment or interest. The teacher subsequently annotated each of the criterion responses with one of three code letters as follows: A — for full understanding achieved, P — for a partial understanding achieved, V — where the work had been no more than 'visited' by the pupil.

It took about a year from the first introduction of this scheme for pupils to learn to use it productively — many at the start wrote very few, and very vague, comments, but during the year these changed and became more explicit and perceptive and so more useful. Pupils were not accustomed to thinking of their own learning as purposeful in relation to target criteria. They also had to break away from treating the assessment as a formal test. Some pupils, especially the less able, did not like to admit failure and sometimes said that they understood when they did not. Teachers tried to emphasize to each pupil that the record was a private document aimed to help the teacher to see the pupil's problems so that help could be given where needed.

In the second school (Fairbrother, 1995) a teacher of physics to a class of 12/13 year-olds wanted them to approach a unit on electricity and magnetism in a more responsible way. He aimed to help them to:

- put each lesson into the context of the whole unit,
- have a summary of what they had been doing for revision purposes,
- see what was to come next in the unit of work.

He gave each pupil a 'revision sheet' for the unit containing about twenty-five short target statements. Most of the pupils had little idea of how to use this list, for example to check the notes in their exercise book against its contents, or to check whether or not they did know what was required. Some of the less-organized pupils simply lost it, others simply stored it away and were not referring to it.

The teacher's explanation of this failure was that these pupils were being given too much teaching about the subject and hardly any teaching about how to learn. The revision sheet was intended to address this issue but the teacher had not realized at the beginning that pupils would need to be taught how to use it. For example, when pupils were told as a homework to 'revise for the test', most of them were floundering. There seemed to be two main reasons for this. The first was that the pupils did not know how to extract, from everything they had done, that which they were supposed to know and understand. Teachers know the difference between the **ends** which they want to achieve and the **means** by which they are trying to achieve them. The pupils do not see this difference. A second reason was that pupils did not know how they would be expected to show their knowledge and understanding. Most pupils learn by experience something of what is required of them, and for many pupils this experience is hard and dispiriting. Some of them, usually the weakest, never do learn.

The above reports make clear that it takes time and patience to achieve a self-assessment capacity because this calls for a radical shift in students' own perspectives about learning. A teacher in Spain reported in very similar terms on the difficulty in achieving this aim:

> The idea of self-evaluation is a difficult one, because the students don't fully comprehend the idea and only really think in terms of their exam mark.

Generally speaking they don't reflect on their own learning process in an overall fashion. [They think] their assessment has more to do with the effort they made than with what they have actually learnt. In fact the main reason why students fail is their lack of study techniques, since they still tend to try to simply memorize things. (Black and Atkin, 1996, p. 99)

Pupils' Expectations

One feature that emerges from these stories is that the expectations that pupils have built up from their experiences of assessment in school can constitute an obstacle to their taking a positive role in assessment. This evidence is further supported in an account of a study of primary pupils in the Geneva Canton (Perrin, 1991). Here, it emerged that the pupils believed that the summative assessments of them were for the school's and their parents' benefit, not for themselves. The weak pupils believed the purpose was to make them work harder. Since the assessment was not used to tell them how to work differently, they saw it as a source of pressure, which made them anxious. As a consequence of such evidence, the canton decided to reduce its summative tests and enhance the formative role of assessment.

Where formative assessment has been emphasized, it has been found that pupils bring to the work a fear of assessment from their experience of summative tests, and it takes some time for them to become more positive about formative work (Black and Dockrell, 1984; Black and Wiliam 1997). They share with teachers a difficulty in converting from norm-referenced to criterion referenced ways of thinking. This matters because as long as pupils compare themselves with others, those with high attainment are too little challenged and those with low attainment are demotivated. The conversion happens more effectively if teachers can give time to setting targets to individual pupils — the ipsative, self-referenced approach seems to be a key here.

Can Pupils Assess Themselves?

The opening stories show that a positive answer can be given to this question, but that it might take time and hard work to develop the capability. There are other studies which show that the answer to this question can be yes: for example, it has also been shown that school pupils can produce valid and reliable evaluation of different styles of the teaching of reading with English literature (Janssen and Rijlaarsdam, 1996). However, they all make clear that hard work is required — to change pupils' own assumptions about how to learn and to change the associated habits in learning that traditional schooling has instilled in them. There is clear evidence that in many cases, pupils lack any clear overview of their learning (Baird and Northfield, 1992), and that where self-assessment is involved, pupils are easily confused because they do not understand the criteria on which to base such assessment (Broadfoot *et al.*, 1988).

Given that pupils must have clear ideas about the purposes of their learning and relate these to criteria which set the bench-marks for the assessment, it follows that they cannot play an effective part in their own assessment except within a long-term programme designed to help them achieve and sustain an overview of their learning targets and to apply the criteria which comprise it to their own progress. An important part of such a programme should be the translation of curriculum aims into language that all pupils can understand, and down to a level of detail that helps them relate directly to their learning efforts.

It also follows that targets have to be both attainable in the short term, and adequately modest in relation to the learners' prospects of success. These requirements come out in particularly sharp form in the teaching of pupils with special learning difficulties — but they are important for all. Any particular learning problem can then be seen as one of closing a gap, between the present attainment and the desired one as specified by the appropriate criterion. If the gap is too large, intermediate criteria have to be provided. The learner needs to understand the gap if she is to cross it; the teacher can help the learner but cannot actually cross it for her. As Sadler (1986) puts it:

> The essential conditions for improvement are that the *student* comes to hold a concept of quality roughly similar to that held by the teacher, is able to monitor continuously the quality of what is being produced *during the act of production itself,* and has a repertoire of alternative moves or strategies from which to draw at any given point. (p. 121)

A study of children in their first four years in primary school asked them to place themselves and their classmates in rank order of good performance in school work (Crocker and Cheeseman, 1988). This yielded high correlations — in the range of 0.6 to 0.8 — between children's self-assessments and assessments by their teachers, between peer assessments and self-assessments and between peer and teacher assessments. This shows that even very young children can assess their teachers' perceptions, of themselves and of their peers, fairly accurately. However, the judgments involved are general judgments of overall success with school work, deriving perhaps from the way that teachers' convey their opinions to children in the classroom. Such judgments are very different from self-assessment with a detailed and effective diagnostic purpose.

Self-assessment, Learning and Meta-cognition

Examples of the Link

In a project on the assessment of the arts, work which started out with a focus on assessment by teachers moved towards development of artistic appreciation by the pupils and ended up as a project on pupils' self assessment. The conclusion of this study was that the teacher's role was to equip the pupil with the reflective skills to master and assess their own work. In their analysis of their findings, the authors of the study (Ross *et al.*, 1993) drew upon the concept of the reflective practitioner, as developed for teachers but now applied to pupils:

> Whilst acknowledging the value of reflection that accompanies and informs production (kinds of formative assessment requiring varying degrees of detachment from making during an ongoing process of production), we have been brought to appreciate, in the course of this research, the singular and remarkable insights that become possible through the various activities subsumed under the heading of what we have called publication — especially in transactions of praise, celebration and judgment. As most of our case studies illustrate, pupils are capable of rich and sophisticated responses to and understandings of their own work and seem well able to develop these responses and understandings in collaboration with their conversation partner. This phase of creative and expressive production in the arts is, we believe, considerably under-represented in most schools' practice and yields a field of opportunity for aesthetic knowing as well as appraisal of enormous potential. (p. 160)

This extract illustrates that in work which is focused on a production by pupils, the appraisal by them is both a process of self-assessment and a part of the learning. This is indeed true of all self-assessment — but the link is more clear than usual in the particular case discussed in the above quotation.

The same emphasis comes out in the development of 'authentic assessment' in the USA. The account by Linda Darling-Hammond *et al.* (1995) emphasized the importance of pupils keeping their own records, and the learning value of a final assessment in which each pupil had to present her work and respond to questions in a personal appearance before an assessment committee. In one school, individual projects were presented before a committee of teachers and other students — a process which was held to be both frightening yet powerful in advancing the student's understanding of his or her learning (p. 94). In another school, students made a report on a whole portfolio of their work to an assessment committee of teachers, who would discuss it with the student, with other students and parents present (p. 56). Stiggins (1994, pp. 209–11) also reviews this approach, including examples where students might present work on a particular project, and where students have been given the responsibility to make individual reports to their own parents' at a parents evening. His book emphasizes at several points the advantage of having pupils participate in the preparation of assessment exercises and in drawing up criteria for scoring them: a particularly striking example is his account of Zola's method for promoting and assessing pupils' participation in discussion (Zola, 1992).

The lessons of this section are amply illustrated by the experience of the Project for Enhanced Effective Learning (PEEL) (Baird and Northfield, 1992). This Australian project was concerned with learning development — as the name suggests — in one school. One teacher described how things were going well until he hit a 'roadblock' — when he told the pupils they were going to have a test. This was because their expectation of a test was that it would be irrelevant to the thinking they were being encouraged to develop. A range of techniques was used to change pupils' views of assessments. One was to give them the opportunity to rework homework so that they could learn from the criticisms of a first marking. Another was to set tests in the middle of a unit so that there was time to learn from them. More radically, students were asked to discuss the marking criteria and then to mark their own or one another's test papers. More radically still, pupils were set the task of devising questions for their test paper, and a selection of such questions made up the paper, which students subsequently marked. This degree of 'ownership' changed the estrangement effect of testing into a lively involvement, and made the test one positive component in the growth of pupils' involvement and reflection on their own learning.

Self-assessment is Intrinsic to Learning

These examples all support a more general argument that in order to become effective as learners, pupils need to progress in their knowledge of themselves as thinkers and learners, in their understanding of particular tasks, and in their strategic knowledge of how to go about the improvement of their own learning (Alexander *et al.*, 1991). It is hard to see how pupils can progress in these dimensions unless they are helped to develop self-assessment. Thus, if effective learning requires that pupils become increasingly involved in taking responsibility for their own learning, then they must also be involved in their own assessment. When an assessment activity is closely built into a learning programme, it would be foolish to prevent pupils from commenting on their results, from challenging them, and from repeating assessments if they so wished to improve their performance. Thus formative assessments should become both informal, and pupil driven, as a consequence of their role in supporting learning.

The capacity of students to judge their own work is more than a bonus in good formative assessment. Self assessment at the point of learning is a crucial component for developing complex understandings through reflect-ive habits of mind (Zessoules and Gardner, 1991). The development of self assessment by pupils is still in its early stages, but within the framework of formative assessment as an integral part of learning, it seems a natural, almost essential development, as well as a potentially powerful source for the im-provement of learning. Indeed, some have argued that meta-cognition, by which they mean awareness and self-direction about the nature of their learning work, is essential to students' development in concept learning, and the work described here is clearly serving that purpose (Brown, 1987; White and Gunstone, 1989; Baird and Northfield, 1992). Thus improved formative assessment can lead to changes which are of much wider significance — changes which should be a powerful help with students' personal develop-ment and which should also be part of any programme to help them to be more effective learners.

Motivation and Self-esteem

A pupil's development as a learner is closely bound up with personal devel-opment as a whole. Jervis (1991) studied a case in which patient work built up supportive yet fragile relationships in an urban classroom in the USA with pupils with learning and behavioural difficulties. He gives a graphic descrip-tion of how the gains were almost destroyed by the threat of the state mandated tests, which brought with them fear and excited old feelings of helplessness and revolt. After the tests, the teacher had to start work again to rebuild the relationships that could support learning. In a similar vein, Werthman (1976) describes how negotiation about the grades they were being awarded was a key determinant in the relationships of disruptive teenagers in a US school.

Thus, pupils' feelings about their learning are key determinants in class-room work. These feelings are built up steadily from their earliest experi-ence of schooling. A disturbing feature of the research reported above on young children's capacity to assess their position in the classroom rank order of good learners is that the weak children may have already begun to accept that they cannot succeed. Reporting on research with children in early prim-ary school years, Sylva (1994) describes the emergence of two types of children — the mastery type and the helpless type. Mastery children:

- are motivated by desire to learn;
- will tackle difficult tasks in flexible and reflective ways;
- are confident of success, believing that they can do it if they try;
- believe that you can improve your intelligence;
- if they see another hard-working child, they will say 'she must be interested'.

By contrast, helpless children:

- are motivated by a desire to be seen to do well;
- seem to accept that they will fail because they just are not clever enough;
- believe that if something seems too hard there is nothing they can do about it;
- tend therefore to avoid any challenge;
- do not believe that they can improve their intelligence.

Membership between the two categories does not appear to be related to a child's intelligence. These different attitudes are seen on a larger scale in differences between cultures. In Asiatic countries, failure to achieve is assumed to be related to lack of hard work. In the USA, and to a lesser extent in other western countries, the belief in innate fixed ability, linked to the use of IQ tests, leads to an assumption that some are predestined to fail (Holloway, 1988). Teachers reflect these assumptions, and can affect children's self-image by the way in which they project them onto children (Black and Wiliam, 1997).

Pupils' motivation to learn is a compound of their intrinsic interest in the work and their desire to succeed at school. The former is stronger with young primary pupils, but is overlaid by the latter as they get older. The research evidence shows that their persistence with a task then depends on how successful they expect to be. Their perceptions of themselves as learners will be dependent on the quality of the feedback that they have experienced over the years. Where it is vague or incomplete, it does not help pupils to know what to do, and it also indicates that their efforts are poor ones, then they will come to believe that they are unable to succeed. Pupils tend to explain their difficulties in terms of effort, or luck, or mood, or teacher bias, and it seems that there can be a world of difference in this respect between their teacher's view of them and their own perceptions (Little, 1985). In order to understand how assessment affects pupils, it is necessary to study their own explanations for their successes and failures, and to be aware that these change with age (Pollard, 1996).

An important aspect here is pupils' self-esteem. This can be enhanced by assessment processes, but it is also easy to inflict damage. Positive self-esteem and high levels of attainment are closely correlated; 'learned helplessness' is the down-side of this same connection (Gipps, 1994, p. 132). Self-esteem is strongly influenced by feedback from peers, parents and teachers. The experience of classroom feedback will affect the way in which children perceive themselves as successful, which will in turn depend on how the teacher responds to their own efforts, and on how a child sees the same teacher's response to others in the class (Crocker and Cheeseman, 1988).

A review of evidence about the teaching styles needed for effective group work illustrated further these general lessons. It showed that the ways in which teachers control, and react to pupils' performances is a delicate and critical factor. Apart from the most able and confident, many pupils are self-protective and will negotiate a level of task which does not expose them to public failure or criticism. Thus, a careful response to their work, in an atmosphere where empathy is established, is essential if challenging and worthwhile tasks are to be tackled (Galton and Williamson, 1992).

All of this emphasizes the importance of teachers' formative assessment being framed in the light of an understanding of pupils' beliefs and feelings, about the feedback process and about the context, of personal relationships and self-esteem, in which it takes place. Such sensitivity involves a study of pupils' motivation, and of the values which interact with motivation, so that teachers can be helped to create a classroom atmosphere which enables pupils to work with confidence at the learning tasks (Raven, 1991).

Scope for Development

This field has been neither researched, nor explored and developed in practice, to any significant extent. Traditional summative practices, and the beliefs instilled in pupils which follow from them, not only miss some very promising opportunities, but actually set up obstacles to better learning. The studies to date do suggest a tremendous potential for improvement through self-assessment. They also suggest that skill in self-assessment might well be essential if other developments essential to better learning — greater personal responsibility, more reflection on one's learning, enhanced self-esteem and motivation — are to bear fruit. A teacher involved in a — very successful — project to improve students' self-assessment in mathematics in Norway expressed all this clearly as follows:

> Pupil self-assessment has a consequence that they are more motivated and conscious in relation to their work. They are more responsible, and their efforts are more long-term and goal-centred. (Black and Atkin, 1996, p. 110).

Summary

- Where pupils are involved in their own assessment, it changes their role as pupils and their relationship with their teachers.
- Most pupils see assessment results as summary indicators of their success; they do not see them as serving their interests and do not look for feedback about how to improve the way that they work.

- In many classrooms, pupils do not perceive the structure of learning aims that gives meaning to the work: because of this, they are unable to assess their own progress against learning criteria.
- There is evidence that pupils can assess themselves if they can see the learning aims clearly and if assessment feedback provides clear information about the gap between their work and achievement of these aims.
- Self-assessment requires a reflective judgment of one's own work; the capacity to make such judgments is an essential and intrinsic feature of effective learning.
- Pupils quickly learn to label themselves as good learners or as helpless; the latter label can demotivate and lead pupils to believe that there is no point in making efforts to learn.
- Good formative assessment has therefore to be ipsative rather than normative, devoted to building self esteem and belief in oneself in every pupil.
- Formative self-assessment can be developed to improve pupils' capacities and will to learn, but pupils' experience of traditional summative practices is an obstacle to such development.

Bibliography

AIRASIAN, P.W. (1991) *Classroom Assessment*, New York: McGraw Hill. Chapters 8 and 10.

BAIRD, J.R. and NORTHFIELD, J.R. (eds) (1992) *Learning from the PEEL Experience*, Melbourne: Monash University.

BLACK, H.D. and DOCKRELL, W.B. (1984) *Criterion Referenced Assessment in the Classroom*, Edinburgh: Scottish Council for Research in Education.

BLACK, P. and ATKIN, J.M. (1996) *Changing the Subject: Innovations in science, mathematics and technology education*, London: Routledge for OECD.

BROADFOOT, P. (1996) 'Assessment and learning: Power or partnership', in GOLDSTEIN, H. and LEWIS, T. (eds) *Assessment: Problems, Developments and Statistical Issues*, Chichester and New York: John Wiley, Chapter 3, pp. 21–40.

CROOKS, T.J. (1988) The impact of classroom evaluation practices on students, *Review of Educational Research*, **58**, 4, pp. 438–481.

DARLING-HAMMOND, L., ANCESS, J. and FALK, B. (1995) *Authentic Assessment in Action Studies of Schools and Students at Work*, New York: Teachers' College Press. A study based upon detailed case-studies of innovations in teachers' assessments in five schools in or near New York.

FAIRBROTHER, R., BLACK, P. and GILL, P. (eds) (1995) *Teachers Assessing Pupils: Lessons from Science Classrooms*, Hatfield UK: Association for Science Education.

GIPPS, C.V. (1994) *Beyond Testing: Towards a Theory of Educational Assessment*, London: Falmer. Chapter 7.

ROSS, M., RADNOR, H., MITCHELL, S. and BIERTON, C. (1993) *Assessing Achievement in the Arts*, Buckingham: Open University Press.

STIGGINS, R.J. (1994) *Student-Centered Classroom Assessment*, New York: Merrill/
Macmillan. Chapters 9 and 15; note also his emphasis on student participation
in test development in Chapters 6 to 8.

WOOD, R. (1991) *Assessment and Testing*, Cambridge: Cambridge University Press.
Chapter 6.

References

ALEXANDER, P.A., SCHALLERT, D.L. and HARE, V.C. (1991) 'Coming to terms: How
researchers in learning and literacy talk about knowledge', *Review of Educational Research*, **62**, 3, pp. 315–43.

BAIRD, J.R. and NORTHFIELD, J.R. (eds) (1992) *Learning from the PEEL Experience*,
Melbourne: Monash University.

BLACK, H.D. and DOCKRELL, W.B. (1984) *Criterion Referenced Assessment in the
Classroom*, Edinburgh: Scottish Council for Research in Education.

BLACK, P. and ATKIN, J.M. (1996) *Changing the Subject: Innovations in Science,
Mathematics and Technology Education*, London: Routledge for OECD.

BLACK, P. and WILIAM, D. (1997) 'Assessment and Classroom Learning', *Assessment
in Education* (in press).

BROADFOOT, P., JAMES, M., MCMEEKING, S., NUTTALL, D. and STIERER, S. (1988) *Records of
Achievement: Report of the National Evaluation of Pilot Schemes*, London: HMSO.

BROWN, A. (1987) 'Metacognition, executive control, self-regulation and other more
mysterious mechanisms', in WEINERT, F.E. and KLUWE, R.H. (eds) *Metacognition,
Motivation and Understanding*, Hillsdale, NJ: Lawrence Erlbaum, pp. 65–116.

CROCKER, A.C. and CHEESEMAN, R.G. (1988) 'The ability of young children to rank
themselves for academic ability', *Educational Studies*, **14**, 1, pp. 105–10.

CROOKS, T.J. (1988) 'The impact of classroom evaluation practices on students',
Review of Educational Research, **58**, 4, pp. 438–81.

DARLING-HAMMOND, L., ANCESS, J. and FALK, B. (1995) *Authentic Assessment in Action:
Studies of Schools and Students at Work*, New York: Teachers' College Press.

FAIRBROTHER, R. (1995) 'Pupils as learners', in FAIRBROTHER, R., BLACK, P. and GILL,
P. (eds) (1995) *Teachers Assessing Pupils: Lessons from Science Classrooms*,
Hatfield: Association for Science Education, pp. 105–24.

GALTON, M. and WILLIAMSON, J. (1992) *Group Work in the Primary Classroom*,
London: Routledge.

GIPPS, C.V. (1994) *Beyond Testing: Towards a Theory of Educational Assessment*,
London: Falmer Press.

HOLLOWAY, S.D. (1988) 'Concepts of ability and effort in Japan and the United States',
Review of Educational Research, **58**, 3, pp. 327–45.

JANSSEN, T. and RIJLAARSDAM, G. (1996) 'Students as self-assessors: Learning experi-
ences of literature teaching in secondary schools', in MARUM, E. (ed.) *Children and
Books in the Modern World: Contemporary Perspectives on Literacy*, London:
Falmer Press, pp. 98–114.

JERVIS, K. (1991) 'Closed gates in a New York City school', in PERONNE, V. (ed.)
Expanding Student Assessment, Alexandria, VA: Association for Supervision
and Curriculum Development, pp. 1–21.

LITTLE, A. (1985) 'The child's understanding of the causes of academic success and failure: A case study of British schoolchildren', *British Journal of Educational Psychology*, **55**, pp. 11–23.

PARKIN, C. and RICHARDS, N. (1995) 'Introducing formative assessment at KS3: An attempt using pupil self-assessment', in FAIRBROTHER, R., BLACK, P. and GILL, P. (eds) (1995) *Teachers Assessing Pupils: Lessons from Science Classrooms*, Hatfield: Association for Science Education, pp. 13–28.

PERRIN, M. (1991) 'Summative evaluation and pupil motivation', in WESTON, P. (ed.) *Assessment of Pupil Achievement: Motivation and School Success*, Amsterdam: Swets and Zeitlinger, pp. 169–73.

POLLARD, A. (1996) 'Pupil perspectives on curriculum, pedagogy and assessment', in CROLL, P. (ed.) *The Social World of Children's Learning*, London: Cassell.

RAVEN, J. (1991) *The Tragic Illusion: Educational Testing*, Oxford: Trillium Press.

ROSS, M., RADNOR, H., MITCHELL, S. and BIERTON, C. (1993) *Assessing Achievement in the Arts*, Buckingham: Open University Press.

SADLER, R. (1989) 'Formative assessment and the design of instructional systems', *Instructional Science*, **18**, pp. 119–44.

STIGGINS, R.J. (1994) *Student-Centred Classroom Assessment*, New York: Merrill/ Macmillan.

SYLVA, K. (1994) 'School influences on children's development', *Journal of Child Psychology and Psychiatry*, **35**, 1, pp. 135–70.

WERTHMAN, C. (1976) 'Delinquents in schools', in BECK, J., JENKS, C., KEDDIE, N. and YOUNG, M.F.D. (eds) *Worlds Apart: Readings for the Sociology of Education*, London: Collier Macmillan, pp. 258–78.

WHITE, R.T. and GUNSTONE, R.E. (1989) 'Meta-learning and conceptual change', *International Journal of Science Education*, **11**, pp. 577–86.

ZESSOULES, R. and GARDNER, H. (1991) 'Authentic assessment: Beyond the buzzword and into the classroom', in PERONNE, V. (ed.) *Expanding Student Assessment*, Alexandria, VA: Association for Supervision and Curriculum Development, pp. 47–71.

ZOLA, J. (1982) 'Middle and high school scored discussions', *Social Education*, **56**, 2, pp. 121–5.

Chapter 9

Certification and Accountability

Introduction

Chapter 3 discussed three main purposes of assessment. The previous two chapters, 7 and 8, have concentrated mainly on the formative purpose. The focus of this chapter will be on the certification and accountability purposes. The first section is concerned with the certification of pupils, supplementing the relevant work in earlier chapters mainly by brief accounts of the systems used in several different countries, leading to a discussion about the significance of the wide variety that has been described. The treatment of accountability is opened with an analysis of the use of the term 'standards' in judgments of quality in education. This leads on naturally to a consideration of the various types of comparisons that are made across different parts of the educational system, and which play an important role in accountability debates.

Certification Varieties

The Story So Far

The general principles relevant to assessment systems serving the purpose of certification of pupils have already been set out in earlier chapters. The main sections are:

- 'Certification, progress and transfer' in Chapter 3.
- 'Summative assessment by teachers' and particularly the sub-section on *Moderation and reliability* in Chapter 7.
- Several sections in Chapter 6 — those on 'Planning and assembling a test', on 'Preparation, analysis and administration', on 'Macro systems, and on 'Portfolios and records'.

The discussion here builds on this basis by giving brief accounts of the combinations of methods used in several countries to assign certificates to students at the end of compulsory teaching or for university selection. It will illustrate a wide variety of practices; this general feature will be discussed further in the ensuing section.

England and Wales

The systems used to award pupils publicly accepted assessment certificates vary widely from one country to another. England and Wales have, at both GCSE and A-levels, a system which uses externally set and marked tests, which include a range of fixed response, closed response and open-ended questions, and adds to these a component of marks, up to 20 per cent, determined by teachers' assessments of particular types of work which are subject to external moderation. For the national assessments at ages 7, 11 and 14, there is no such addition — the teachers' assessments and the external test results are reported separately.

Sweden

In Sweden, external final examinations were abandoned in 1971 and replaced by school assessments. There are national tests in some subjects, but these are used to calibrate teachers' own assessments. The mean and range of marks in the national tests of a particular school determine a mean and spread to which its final results must conform, but the school is free to use its own results, together with the national test results, to determine awards for individual pupils within this constraint. However, there are national constraints on teachers' record keeping and on procedures for aligning the external and internal summative results (Broadfoot *et al.*, 1990, pp. 93–4; Eckstein and Noah, 1993, pp. 36–40).

Federal Germany

Systems generally have a different character in countries with strong regional governments where education is a regional rather than a federal responsibility. There is significant variety in Germany between the different regions (or *lander*). All those who are hoping for university entrance — about 40 per cent of the age cohort — attempt the *Abitur* certificate assessment. This is based on results in four subjects, with coursework grades contributing 64 per cent of the marks and final written examinations the balance. Written papers are taken in three of the four subjects, the other being assessed by an oral examination. In some regions, the written papers are externally set and the same for all pupils, but in others they are set for their own school by the teachers in that school, although they have to submit their questions for central approval. Overall there is pressure because the universities, which used to allow open access, now have to restrict access. They believe that the standards differ between the different *lander* and so make their own allowances for this, and for the more popular disciplines they also require additional tests and interviews (Britton and Raizen, 1996, pp. 224–233).

Japan

The pressure for university entrance is an even more dominant feature in Japan, where university examinations are the only school leaving examination. There is a common, national, entrance examination, which is based almost entirely on fixed response test items (Broadfoot *et al.*, 1990, pp. 87–8). Those who do sufficiently well in this examination then have to take a second examination if they wish to enter for any university of high prestige — the higher the prestige, the more searching the examination. These second stage examinations are set separately by each university and the universities collaborate to make them available on only two fixed occasions per year, so that a pupil may only enter for two universities. This process is expensive for families — the fees for each examination are high (some universities make a useful profit from them) and there is also the cost of travel to the university and residence there for two days. These costs have to be paid by the pupil's parents, who will also, in most cases, be paying fees for private education in 'crammer' schools which operate outside the state school hours.

France

Different pressures have affected the French *baccalaureat* examination. This was started in 1806, in the Napoleonic era, as an elite examination which came to guarantee entrance to higher education. Even up to the 1950s it only catered for a small minority with an academic emphasis and covering only four subject areas. Since than it has been reformed in an attempt to make it a qualification for all — so that in 1992, 51 per cent of the age group were entering, with choice across thirty-eight subject areas within three main types of *baccalaureat*, academic, technical, and professional. The examination is mainly written, but with an oral component, and any one pupil will be subject to about twenty-five hours of examination. The growth in the examination has also led to the original national organization being replaced by a set of regional organizations, with each region setting, marking and grading its own papers. There have been attempts at introducing strong components of teacher assessment, with keen support from some teachers. However, teachers' demands for recognition of the extra work load in their employment conditions has clouded this enthusiasm. The high status of the examination as anonymous, fair, and independent of bias or of schools' high or low reputations, has meant that its continuation as a solely external test commands support from parents, pupils and some teachers (Broadfoot, 1996, Chapter 6).

Australia

The states of Australia each have their own system. The state of Queensland abandoned state-wide examinations in 1982 and left pupils' certification in the hands of schools. The underlying purpose was to strengthen the formative–summative link and to move to a criterion referenced basis. When it was realized that schools were not moving in these directions, but were instead setting their own local versions of the former state tests, a further programme of teacher development had to be set up. Schools now work in regional groups, and the teachers' assessment methods and their graded results have to be exchanged and justified in meetings of these groups in order to ensure comparability of standards (Butler, 1995). Other countries, including developing countries, have tried to enhance the use of continuous assessment by teachers but have encountered severe difficulties because of the lack of expertise amongst teachers, the extra work loads on them, and fears of bias and corruption (Pennycuick, 1990; Greaney and Kellaghan, 1996).

Bewildering Varieties

In the case of a large country with a single national system it would be costly and administratively cumbersome to operate, on a national basis, any system using teachers' assessmens, so it is not surprising that the national university entrance test in China, which has to handle about 1.7 million candidates each year, uses only paper tests, now with substantial multiple choice elements (Lewin and Wang Lu, 1990).

The inventory of different examination systems and practices expands further as more countries are studied. Two further examples will suffice. Hungary has a book of over 1000 test questions for (say) physics in use in every school — on the day of the physics examination the numbers of the questions selected for that year's test are read out over the television and pupils can find the questions in the book and answer them (Gecso, 1993).

In Poland, the examination for university entrance comprises written tests in two subjects and oral examinations in three more. The written papers and guidelines for the orals are prescribed nationally, but the marking of the papers and the conduct and marking of the orals are left to the school. For a typical oral examination, each pupil will be given a set of possible questions about an hour before his oral and will be able to think about these, in examination conditions, before the questioning begins. Here is an account by a physics examiner of the reasons for using orals (which constitute the only examination in physics):

> Orals are used not only through adherence to tradition, but because many teachers believe that only in oral examinations can an examiner trace the student's thoughts and react by asking further questions. In an oral, it is possible to explore, in a unique way, the student's ability to communicate, to formulate his thoughts, to describe and explain physical phenomena, and to explain how and why new concepts and laws are established. In short, even although the difficulty of ensuring objectivity in examinations is recognized, there is a general belief that the depth of enquiry and the personal interaction that are unique to orals make them an indispensable method for assessment. (Plazak and Mazur, 1993)

Understanding Variety

The bewildering variety can be interpreted as a sign of two underlying determinants. The first is the extent to which a society judges that teachers could or should be involved in examining for certification of their own pupils. There is a variety of ways in which their assessments contribute to the result: it can be seen that their contribution can range from:

- being the sole and entire source;
- being the sole source but with their results nationally calibrated;
- being the sole source uncalibrated but with their methods checked;
- providing results which are combined with external tests to give a single result;
- providing results which are set alongside external test results but not combined;
- having no role at all except to help their pupils to meet the external test.

Issues of cost, of size of the regional or national unit, and of the status and trust which teachers can command, all bear on such choices. However, the variety can also be interpreted as signs of discomfort over the dilemma of whether or not to trust teachers — each method being seen as a compromise, sometimes an uneasy one.

Within external testing, there is also a wide range of methods in use. All of these choices and combinations encounter difficulties, principally in reliability, in validity, in cost, and in their effects back on teaching and learning practices. Thus, if anyone were able to abandon current practices and design an entirely new system, they could not conclude that there exists a universal technical optimum and the balance of advantages and problems that their choices exhibited would be evidence of their particular system of values as well as of their technical and educational insights (Creswell, 1996).

The second underlying determinant is the historical and cultural tradition of each country or region. Here the argument returns to the points illustrated in the brief historical studies in Chapter 2. Examination systems cannot be seen as technical structures which can be optimized through objective and rational analysis. They are deeply embedded in the social mores and assumptions of their countries. Those who want to maintain social elites and those who want to break their power, those who want to enhance the status of teachers and those who want to denigrate them, those who already control the selection of the best school leavers and those who want to place that control in different hands, will all be in contest as examining systems are up for renewal or reform. Thus a deeper understanding of the systems has to be based on historical and sociological analysis of each country (Broadfoot, 1996, Chapters 6, 7 and 8 present a detailed comparison between England and France).

Accountability, Quality and Standards

All those responsible for education will claim to be committed to high standards. The term 'standards' is an important slogan, and like all slogans, it can distort debate by attaching restricted meanings to an attractive banner (Gipps and Stobart, 1993, pp. 27–30). Many of the issues involved here have already been explored in the section on 'Grades, cut scores and standards' in Chapter 5. That discussion made clear that the use of the term 'standards' in the public rhetoric can hide several ambiguities and evade difficult technical problems. To summarize some of those points:

- A standard can relate to a criterion score on a test; both the methods of scoring and the decision about setting the criterion level depend on somebody's judgment of what is satisfactory, or of what constitutes a 'high' or (worse still) a 'world-class' standard.
- A 'high' standard could refer to the height of the hurdle or to the proportion of students who can jump it, and there is an obvious trade-off between these two. A common restriction of meaning is to equate high standards with test performance.
- A 'national standard' might be a minimum of performance that all should attain, or a scale of performance levels on which each individual will be placed. Recent documents proposing national standards in the USA imply that all pupils should attain what they propose; this seems unrealistic, but it would weaken the political and rhetorical purposes of the documents to admit that one could aim for less than 100 per cent achievement.

The discussion in this section takes the argument further by considering a broader agenda for any standards debate. For policy guidance, test scores are not the only criterion. For example, there might be a trade-off between different types of standards: Japan was one of the highest scoring countries in recent international comparison tests for science at age 13, but produced one of the lowest proportions of pupils saying that they liked science — which 'standard' is the desirable goal? (Beaton *et al.*, 1996(a)). Thus, even if the debate is limited to output standards, these standards must ultimately refer to judgments of the quality of performance and to value judgments as between different outcome criteria. For example, if curricula change to give more emphasis to thinking about the content and to applying knowledge, then less content might be covered. It would then be easy to set tests on the old basis — which would show that standards had declined, or on the new, which would show that they had changed in character. The judgment between the two could not be quantitative, it would be a value judgment of the relative quality of the different types of outcome.

The indices of high standards for schools and for school systems could be broadened in other directions. Low truancy rates, involvement in out-of-school activities, and high rates of continuation in education after the compulsory age are examples of such indicators. In a carefully argued article about educational reform, a senior officer in the US Federal Department of Education sets out the following three components for a standards debate (O'Day and Smith, 1993):

- Resource standards
  For these, policy should focus on those aspects of school resources, notably the quality of the teachers, which are central to quality work.
- Standards of practice
  Under this heading the focus is mainly on the quality of classroom work. This includes in particular the provision to pupils of opportunity to learn the agreed national and regional components of a curriculum; it is well established — but not surprising — that opportunity to learn is one of the important determinants of pupils' performance and equity principles require that all pupils be given such opportunities in respect of all agreed aspects of the curriculum.
- Performance standards
  These are the various measures of outcome already discussed above.

For each of these, there is need for a careful discussion of what constitutes quality. If a national debate on standards is to serve as an occasion to reformulate policy, it cannot be effective if the focus is placed on only one or two of these three aspects. In relation to the public accountability of schools, this broadening of the standards debate makes clear that pupils, and schools, should be accountable for those features which are under their control, and that others with responsibility in the education system should also be accountable for the quality of their fulfilment of their roles.

An important dilemma is whether any drive to common national standards of expectation will lead to creation of a strait-jacket for schools, which must in the long run suppress the creativity, freedom and status of teachers, and so will inevitably lead to lower standards of performance. A further aspect of this dilemma is exemplified by the development in the UK, which has its counterparts in several other countries, towards 'competence based assessment' (Wolf, 1995). One emphasis in this movement is that the needs of future employers should be given more priority, so that assessment has to be criterion referenced with clearly documented criteria which employers help to determine, and which will focus on general skills rather than on particular curriculum content. This leads to a criterion referenced system, ideally with criteria which are not negotiable in terms of the skills and capabilities that they demand, but which can be realized through courses which may vary in both their structure and in their contents. The underlying issue here is whether a philosophy of content-free standards is viable. The attraction is that it can set up a clear national 'currency' of certification without stifling the creativity of teachers and institutions in composing their own courses. The uncertainty lies in whether such a system can gain the public and political acceptance necessary for its survival. The philosophy has been the basis of the development of National Vocational Qualifications in England and Wales, which has had to struggle with all the difficulties associated with criterion-referencing. The NVQ approach has been to approve institutions to conduct their own assessments based on course-work, but the fact that there has been pressure to introduce external components is a sign of uncertainty in public acceptance.

Comparisons Are Odious

Comparability of standards is also of great interest to politicians and the public, whether the comparisons are over time, or between countries, or between schools, or between individual teachers. The fascination of such exercises is such that there is little prospect of Swift's comment to Sheridan 'But then, comparisons are odious' being heeded. However, if they are not odious, most comparisons can at least be seriously misleading unless made with great care.

Things Ain't What They Used to Be

Comparisons over time are a case in point. Because the curriculum, teaching methods, and assessment methods all change with time, any simple comparison over, say ten years is almost impossible to make. It is possible to set the same questions to pupils and compare their scores, but even if these are questions on a topic that was in the curriculum at both of the times to be compared, the relative emphasis given to that topic may have changed over the years, and the match between the context and style of the questions and the way they been studied in schools may also have changed. In one detailed research study, Christie and Forrest (1980) tried to assess for changes over time in two A-level subjects. Syllabuses, questions, pupils' examination scripts and the marking schemes were used, but the researchers' main conclusion was that it was not possible to make a comparison (Nuttall, 1986). This has not of course prevented others from deploring falling standards on the basis of anecdote, or in defiance of such evidence as can be assembled (Foxman *et al.*, 1993).

Comparing Standards Between Examining Boards

Comparisons of today's standards across different examining agencies examining the same subject present rather similar problems. The different examining groups in England do still examine with different styles and with significant differences between their syllabuses, so that any direct comparisons have to be, in the end, qualitative judgments by experts who have looked at all relevant aspects — syllabuses, papers, mark schemes, scripts and grading standards. Cross-moderation, in which examiners from the two groups compare their data and procedures has been used. Indirect comparisons have been made by the following means. A special sample of students must be selected who:

> have all taken one subject (say subject A) with one group, and some of whom have taken another subject (B) with the same group whilst the rest of them have taken B with another group.

The results in subject A are used as a calibrating reference; thus one can see whether or not, on average, those with the same results in A gain different average results in B between the two boards. However, this method is only justified if the two groups of students are equivalent in the way in which their performances between the reference (A) and the comparison (B) subjects are correlated (technically, if the regression lines of one set of grades on the other are parallel) (Goldstein, 1986; Creswell, 1996). This may not be true, and indeed, one reason why schools enter their students for different group's examinations is because the particular and different emphases of one group in a particular subject are a better match to their students and their methods of teaching than those of other groups.

Comparing Different Subjects

Comparisons between different subjects also bristle with technical difficulties. In principle of course equating a result in (say) English with a result in
physics is like trying to compare butter with apples. It is possible to explore
whether pupils with the same 'ability' do equally well in the two subjects,
but this involves unjustifiable assumptions about equality of 'ability' in relation to two different subjects. Comparisons are made in two main ways. One
is to compare the mean scores in any two subjects between all who have
taken the same examinations. More complex statistical procedures explore
all such pair-wise combinations across all of the GCSE or all of the A-level
subjects taken by a population. Another way applied to A-levels has been to
take a common predictor, the GCSE results across all of their subjects of the
students two years earlier, and explore how students with the same overall
GCSE performances succeed at the various A-level subjects. The two approaches have produced comparable results. For example, it is now fairly
clear from such evidence that if two sets of students with comparable GCSE
results enter for A-levels in physics and in English, their A-level grades in
physics will on average be one grade lower than their results in English
(Fitz-Gibbon, 1996, Chapter 15). This last set of comparisons has led to calls
for change in the grading standards between different A-level subjects. This
method of comparison is also the basis of an A-level Information Service for
schools (the ALIS system) which supplies predictions of A-level grades on
the basis of GCSE performance.

Comparing Schools — The League Tables

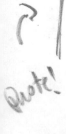

More highly charged politically are comparisons made between schools on
the basis of examination or national test results. As pointed out in the section
on 'Accountability' in Chapter 3, such comparisons can be both unfair and
misleading. Whilst the quality of what a school provides does undoubtedly
make a difference to its outcome performance, the attainments of pupils
entering a school is still the single most important determinant of their later
performance. Statistical measures which correct for the performance levels
of their intake can provide 'value-added' measures which could give fairer
comparisons, particularly for secondary schools. However, the ranking of
schools by this means can be altered by making the corrections in different
ways. It may also be the case that different schools may do better for different types of pupils — to explore this requires a more sophisticated analysis
which can separate out effects for different groups of pupils within and
across different schools (Gipps and Stobart, 1993, Chapter 4; Gray, 1996;
Goldstein, 1996). The comparison of standards here can be a trap because,
as pointed out above, it can limit the debate to outcome standards and lead

to the neglect of policy focus on the equally important standards pertaining to resources and to school practices. Given all of these complications, an approach far more comprehensive than that of crude league tables, based on a wide range of performance indicators, is needed if school comparisons are to be both meaningful and helpful in assisting parents to judge which school would be best for their particular child.

The International Horse-race

The final level of comparison is that between countries. The use of tests to make comparisons between countries started in 1962 with a survey of mathematics (McLean, 1990). This was then extended to cover six more subjects. A second round of surveys followed in the 1980s, covering mathematics, science, written composition and classroom environments and known by the acronym SIMSS (second international mathematics and science survey). The international interest in these enabled the organization responsible — the International Association for the Evaluation of Educational Achievement (IEA) to mount a third study (TIMSS) in the early 1990s. The surveys are based on sampling, and on testing frameworks which have to be agreed by international negotiation. Whilst these exercises gave emphasis to the 'league table' position of countries in the overall scores, emphasis has been shifting towards information which is more interpretable for policy purposes. Thus, the collection of related variables, and analysis of results in relation to them, has become more important and the first reports analyse results in many ways and in respect of different aspects of the test data (Beaton *et al.*, 1996(a); 1996(b)). A key determinant is the 'opportunity to learn' the knowledge and skills tested by any particular question. In the TIMSS a very large body of data about curriculum guidelines and textbooks has been collected from about forty-five countries. Analyses of these data for six of these has already shown very large variations in the 'opportunity to learn' variable and the extent to which these variations can account for the score variations between countries remains to be seen (Schmidt *et al.*, 1996, 1997). The trend is to move away from comparisons in terms of a single score, to presentation of a 'snapshot' of the distinctive features of each individual country, within which the scores will contribute one aspect of the total picture. For example, each country's results are now analysed both in respect of the total of the items taken by all, and in relation to those items for which the pupils in that country will have had adequate opportunity to learn at the time of the tests.

National Surveys

National surveys have been discussed in some detail in the section on 'Survey approaches' in Chapter 6. As pointed out there, the intention that surveys can help identify causes of performance variations by collection and analysis of data on related variables is hard to realize, and the data can easily lead to misleading interpretations. Where, within a matrix light sampling strategy, they can develop and disseminate a range of instruments and procedures of high quality, they can help to raise the general level of assessment work, and give useful detailed information to teachers. One of the hopes, that such surveys can reveal changes over time, is hard to realize for all of the reasons already discussed earlier in this section.

Dangerous Simplicities

The overall message is that, whilst it may be over-stating the case to say that comparisons are odious, it is certain that they have to be formulated and interpreted with great care. The lesson emerging from all debates about comparative exercises and surveys is that only complex data requiring sophisticated judgments should command attention. One of those involved in national and international comparison studies speaks about his dilemmas as follows:

> But schooling *is* too complex to control from the centre; it is even too complex to understand from the centre. Cross-national studies have documented this in thousands of ways, but the lure of the simple answer is too strong. Always the pressure is too great to resist, and the diverse results are squeezed, Procrustes-like, into a few simple tables. All the caveats are skimmed over, the qualifications watered down or removed and the generalizations produced. The present writer is as guilty as any. (McLean, 1990, p. 75)

Summary

- The systems used for pupil certification show a wide variety across different countries, particularly in the ways in which teachers' assessments are used in combination with externally set tests.
- This variety is a product of historical practices, and of conflicting technical and educational considerations which are appraised in the light of cultural and social norms.
- The term 'standards' is open to several interpretations: it is ambiguous even if applied only to learning outcomes, and should be broadened to encompass other outcomes and to include standards of quality in educational resources and in classroom practices.
- Comparisons of standards are attempted between different times, different testing agencies, different subjects, different schools, different countries, and within any one country, between different types of institutions or different regions.

- All such comparisons bristle with conceptual and technical problems, so that they call for sophisticated interpretation — which those who make much of them are often unwilling or unable to exercise.

Bibliography

BRITTON, E.D. and RAIZEN, S.A. (1996) *Examining the Examinations: An International Comparison of Science and Mathematics Examinations for College Bound Students*, Boston and Dordrecht: Kluwer.

BROADFOOT, P.M. (1996) *Education, Assessment and Society; A Sociological Analysis*, Buckingham: Open University Press.

BROADFOOT, P., MURPHY, R. and TORRANCE, H. (eds) (1990) *Changing Educational Assessment: International Perspectives and Trends*, London: Routledge.

ECKSTEIN, M.A. and NOAH, H.J. (1993) *Secondary School Examinations: International Perspectives on Policies and Practice*, New Haven: Yale University Press.

GIPPS, C.V. and STOBART, G. (1993) *Assessment: A Teachers' Guide to the Issues*, (2nd. edn.), London: Hodder and Stoughton. Chapters 3, 4 and 8.

GOLDSTEIN, H. and LEWIS, T. (eds) (1996) *Assessment: Problems, Developments and Statistical Issues*, Chichester and New York: John Wiley.

HARLEN, W. (ed.) (1994) *Enhancing Quality in Assessment*, London: Paul Chapman. Chapters 1 and 2.

References

BEATON, A.E. and FIVE OTHERS (1996a) *Science Achievement in the Middle School: IEA's Third International Mathematics and Science Survey*, Chestnut Hill, MA: TIMSS/Boston College.

BEATON, A.E. and FIVE OTHERS (1996b) *Mathematics Achievement in the Middle School: IEA's Third International Mathematics and Science Survey*, Chestnut Hill, MA: TIMSS/Boston College.

BLACK, P.J. (ed.) (1993) *Physics Examinations for University Entrance: An International Study*, Science and Technology Education Document Series No. 45, Paris: UNESCO.

BRITTON, E.D. and RAIZEN, S.A. (eds) (1996) *Examining the Examinations — An International Comparison of Science and Mathematics Examinations for College-bound Students*, Dordrecht and Norwell, MA: Kluwer.

BROADFOOT, P. (1996) *Education, Assessment and Society: A Sociological Analysis*, Buckingham: Open University Press.

BROADFOOT, P., MURPHY, R. and TORRANCE, H. (eds) (1990) *Changing Educational Assessment: International Perspectives and Trends*, London: Routledge.

BUTLER, J. (1995) 'Teachers judging standards in senior science subjects: Fifteen years of the Queensland Experiment', *Studies in Science Education*, **26**, pp. 135–57.

CHRISTIE, T. and FORREST, G.M. (1980) *Standards at GCE A-level 1963 and 1973*, London: Macmillan.

CRESWELL, M.J. (1996) 'Defining, setting and maintaining standards in curriculum-embedded examinations: Judgemental and statistical approaches', in GOLDSTEIN, H. and LEWIS, T. (eds) *Assessment: Problems, Developments and Statistical Issues*, Chichester and New York: Wiley, pp. 57–84.

ECKSTEIN, M.A. and NOAH, H.J. (1993) *Secondary School Examinations: International Perspectives on Policies and Practice*, New Haven: Yale University Press.

FITZ-GIBBON, G.T. (1996) *Monitoring Education : Indicators, Quality and Effectiveness*, London: Cassell.

FOXMAN, D., GORMAN, T. and BROOKS, G. (1993) 'Standards in literacy and numeracy', in *National Commission on Education Briefings*, London: Heinemann, pp. 135–50.

GECSO, E. (1993) 'National entrance examinations in Hungary', in BLACK, P.J. (ed.) *Physics Examinations for University Entrance: An International Study*, Science and Technology Education Document Series No. 45, Paris; UNESCO, pp. 85–100.

GIPPS, C.V. and STOBART, G. (1993) *Assessment: A Teachers' Guide to the Issues*, 2nd edition, London: Hodder and Stoughton.

GOLDSTEIN, H. (1986) 'Methods for equating test scores and for studying the comparability of public examinations', in NUTTALL, D.L. (ed.) *Assessing Educational Achievement*, London: Falmer Press, pp. 168–84.

GOLDSTEIN, H. (1996) 'The statistical analysis of institution based data', in GOLDSTEIN, H. and LEWIS, T. (eds) *Assessment: Problems, Developments and Statistical Issues*, Chichester and New York: Wiley, pp. 135–44.

GOLDSTEIN, H. and LEWIS, T. (eds) (1996) *Assessment: Problems, Developments and Statistical Issues*, Chichester and New York: Wiley.

GRAY, J. (1996) 'The use of assessment to compare institutions', in GOLDSTEIN, H. and LEWIS, T. (eds) *Assessment Problems: Developments and Statistical Issues*, Chichester and New York: John Wiley, pp. 121–33.

GREANEY, V. and KELLAGHAN, T. (1996) 'The integrity of public examinations in developing countries', in GOLDSTEIN, H. and LEWIS, T. (eds) *Assessment: Problems, Developments and Statistical Issues*, Chichester and New York: John Wiley, pp. 167–88.

LEWIN, K. and WANG, LU. (1990) 'University entrance examination in China: A quiet revolution', in BROADFOOT, P., MURPHY, R. and TORRANCE, H. (eds) *Changing Educational Assessment: International Perspectives and Trends*, London: Routledge, pp. 153–76.

McLEAN, L. (1990) 'Possibilities and limitations in cross-national comparisons of educational achievement', in BROADFOOT, P., MURPHY, R. and TORRANCE, H. (eds) *Changing Educational Assessment: International Perspectives and Trends*, London: Routledge, pp. 65–83.

NUTTALL, D.L. (ed.) (1986) *Assessing Educational Achievement*, London: Falmer Press.

NUTTALL, D.L. (1986) 'Problems in the measurement of change', in NUTTALL, D.L. (ed.) *Assessing Educational Achievement*, London: Falmer Press, pp. 153–67.

O'DAY, J.A. and SMITH, M.S. (1993) 'Systemic reform and educational opportunity', in FUHRMAN, S. (ed.) *Designing Coherent Policy: Improving the System*, San Francisco: Jossey Bass, pp. 250–312. At the time of writing Marshall Smith is Under-Secretary of State for Education in the US Department of Education.

PENNYCUICK, D. (1990) 'The introduction of continuous assessment systems at secondary level in developing countries', in BROADFOOT, P., MURPHY, R. and TORRANCE, H. (eds) *Changing Educational Assessment: International Perspectives and Trends*, London: Routledge, pp. 106–18.

PLAZAK, T. and MAZUR, Z. (1993) 'University entrance in Poland', in BLACK, P.J. (ed.) Physics Examinations for University Entrance: An International Study, Science and Technology Education Document Series No. 45, Paris: UNESCO, pp. 125–39.

SCHMIDT, W.H. and FOURTEEN OTHERS (1996) *Characterizing Pedagogical Flow: An Investigation of Mathematics and Science Teaching in Six Countries*, Dordrecht: Kluwer.

SCHMIDT, W.H., McKNIGHT, C.C., VALVERDE, G.A., HOUANG, R.T. and WILEY, D.E. (1997) *Many Visions, Many Aims Volume I: A Cross-National Investigation of Curricular Intentions in Mathematics*, Dordrecht and Boston: Kluwer.

WOLF, A. (1995) *Competence Based Assessment*, Buckingham: Open University Press.

WOODHOUSE, G. and GOLDSTEIN, H. (1996) 'The statistical analysis of institution–based data', in GOLDSTEIN, H. and LEWIS, T. (ed.) *Assessment: Problems, Developments and Statistical Issues*, Chichester and New York: John Wiley, pp. 135–44.

Chapter 10

Conclusions

Friend or Foe?

The answer to this question will be a mixed one. The alternatives can be examined in relation to the three main purposes that assessment serves. As an essential element of any learning programme, formative assessment must be a friend. Because anyone with educated capabilities requires proof of their achievements, summative individual assessment will always be essential, but the effort required for its attainment may strain any affection for the process. Since the public good requires accountability, this function is also inescapable — although we may have no more love for its necessity than we have for paying taxes. Altogether, the best that might be achieved lies between affection and indifference. But if the system as a whole is ill-designed, hostility may be the only option.

Assessment and testing will inevitably be areas of contention. The main reasons for this have been explored throughout this book. They are:

- Assessment and testing are important guard posts on the boundary between the internal work of schools and the public interest in control of that work.
- Assessment issues are not marginal features of education — they are central.
- The assessment and testing practices which any of us experience are a product of our particular historical and social contexts: this insight might help us to understand them better, but it will also warn us that the practices cannot easily be changed.
- Assessment practices cannot stand still — they are driven by social changes and can be used to promote or resist those changes. A notable case is the need to move from higher education for an elite to mass higher education, with the consequent erosion of the dominance of special interests, whether of university entrance, or of particular professions, or of other social elites.
- At the same time, there are other professional pressures to change, notably the moves towards criterion-referencing and away from norm-referencing, towards achieving a better match between learning aims and testing realities, towards assessing an increasingly

broad range of outcomes and personal qualities, and towards giving teachers an enhanced role in assessment.

- The structure of assessment and testing policies is a complex one, involving the intersection of aspects of psychology, pedagogy, curriculum, statistics, professional competence and status, budgets and competing public and political priorities.

Thus there are strong drives for change, but policy cannot move down a broad smooth road. The metaphor is rather of negotiating a mountain pass.

A Rocky Road

The metaphor — evoking negotiation of tight bends, the risk of precipitous falls, the juggernaut coming the other way — seems a little dramatic. If it is justified, this is because any policy faces several obstacles and dilemmas all of which are difficult to overcome or resolve. Seven of the main obstacles which have been explored across the chapters of this book may be summarized as follows:

- *Chapter 2: No educational system can move too far and too fast from its starting point*

Even if we can be freed from old assumptions and can think ourselves into new frameworks, we are still constrained by history and tradition, for all studies of educational change show that attempts to move quickly are counterproductive — they fail and give reform a bad name.

- *Chapter 3: The different purposes are bound to be in tension*

A strong drive for accountability can undermine good practices for certification, for example by requiring a uniformity that inhibits change and by emphasizing reliability at the expense of validity. Policies focused on the accountability and certification functions which pay no heed to their effect on classroom learning will inevitably damage formative assessment. The different purposes, pursued in isolation, pull in contrary directions, not least because they involve debate between those whose interests are bureaucratic, those caring for the professional status and conditions of teachers, and those whose concerns are centred on the strengthening of the pupil. Optimum resolutions are hard to find, but must be pursued.

- *Chapters 4 and 5: Validity is central yet hard to attain*

Achieving information of a quality which will justify the inferences and actions which must be based upon it — i.e. valid information — is notoriously hard to achieve. If this information is to be generated cheaply, we have to use test situations which are so bizarrely unlike those in which people have to use their learned competencies that the task seems almost impossible. Yet it is hard to prove that hallowed practices are both strange and harmful, even harder to justify the cost of doing better. Even without such constraints, far more work is needed to explore the extent to which any known assessment practices can in fact be justified — in the light of the way the results are to be expressed, in the way they are to be understood as meaningful indicators of performance, and in the way they are to be used, both to influence teaching and learning and to select or predict for students' futures. Such justifications are notably lacking at present.

- *Chapter 6: A wide variety of methods is available, but can we afford to use them?*

All methods have their advantages and disadvantages. A system which uses a range of methods can give a rich picture of pupils which, with careful interpretation, can be robust against various sources of random error and of bias. However, such richness has a high cost, which raises the question of priorities — how much are we prepared to pay for better assessment, both in cash and in relaxing other restrictions that are placed on its practices?

- *Chapter 7: Teachers and schools need the freedom of diversity, society needs uniformity*

Teachers are the key to any change, and assessment practices cannot improve unless teachers can be supported by programmes to develop their assessment expertise. Given such programmes, more can be achieved if the status of teachers can be recognized and their expertise trusted. However, this cannot go far if they do not have freedom of manoeuvre, so a tension will arise between imposed uniformity and local autonomy, a tension which will inhere in matters of curriculum, assessment criteria, assessment standards, and the currency of qualifications.

- *Chapter 8: Pupils' expectations are crucial to the learning society*

Building up the capability of pupils is the ultimate goal in education, and assessment is more than a useful adjunct for this task. Much of current thinking about the future of social, business and industrial organizations is moving away from centrally controlled and unchanging structures to 'flat management' structures, which are more adaptable because they can learn quickly and in which responsibility is increasingly delegated to those 'on the ground'. The following extract is an example:

> (M)aking continual learning a way of organizational life . . . can only be achieved by breaking with the traditional authoritarian, command and control hierarchy where the top thinks and the local acts, to merge thinking and acting at all levels. This represents a profound re-orientation in the concerns of management — a shift from a predominant concern with controlling to a predominant concern with learning. (Darling-Hammond *et al.* (1995) quotation from Senge on p. 256)

If pupils are to be prepared for such a society, responsibility for their own learning, and self-assessment so that they can monitor and so control and improve their work outside the protective and supportive framework of the school, will be aims deserving increased priority. Yet to focus on this type of enhancement of pupils' learning takes time and new pedagogy, and less of the content curriculum will be covered. How can teachers be brave enough to do this, and how can external high stakes assessment support them?

- *Chapter 9: Public concerns about standards can be fuelled and misled by simplistic interpretations of test scores*

Raw score data cannot give meaningful and trustworthy comparisons unless they are judged in the contexts of comprehensive data on the many factors which affect such scores, and sophisticated analyses upon which careful evaluations of the data can be based. A particularly salient feature here is the variation in the extent to which different societies feel able to trust and support teachers in playing an important part in assessments for pupil certification and for accountability.

Systemic Strategies: The Scope and the Pace of Change

Improved learning requires thoughtful reflection, discussion, interaction between teachers and taught, and formative feedback. It follows that reform of curriculum, of pedagogy and of formative assessment all have to go together — reform of assessment cannot proceed on its own. Certification and accountability policies should be as consistent with and as supportive of such a reform as possible, yet the fact that all countries seem to compromise in trying to reconcile different purposes and functions is a sure sign that there are no easy solutions. Thus, it is hard to proceed by small steps, yet too risky to try to change everything at once.

Any significant improvement in assessment practices must be supported, if not initiated, by political policies and one strategic priority of such policies must be to achieve optimum consistency between the curriculum, pedagogy and the different purposes which assessment should serve. Thus, reform has to be systemic in design, even if it may be piecemeal in implementation. Political strategies are bound to be affected by the understanding of assessment issues, on the part both of politicians and of the general public to whom they must appeal. The following quotation by Shepard (1992, p. 301) talking about the need for reform of assessment policies in the USA could well apply to most other countries:

> If they are unaware of new research findings about how children learn, policy makers are apt to rely on their own implicit theories which were most probably shaped by the theories that were current when they themselves attended school . . . Some things that psychologists can prove today even contradict the popular wisdom of several decades ago. Therefore, if policy makers proceed to implement outmoded theories or tests based on old theories, they might actually subvert their intended goal — of providing a rigorous and high quality education for all students.

Many of the issues in assessment which are discussed in this book are not well understood either by teachers or by educational administrators. A notable example is the very limited reliability of external tests, which command a degree of confidence which they do not deserve, to the detriment of alternative methods. Yet the formulation of effective policies would require difficult and complex decisions even by a group who understood the intricacies and implications involved, and who had struggled through these to a vision of a feasible and yet much improved policy.

Where educational change must touch the core of day to day professional practice, there are further dilemmas about the scope and pace of change. There are expressed in the following extracts from a recent international study of educational innovation and change:

> Classroom pedagogy takes place in a complex ecology of beliefs and values, held differently and in different ways by pupils, parents, teachers and administrators. The systemic approach to reform is becoming common because it recognizes and responds to this complexity. . . . If you want to avoid discontinuities, unanticipated tensions and un-met needs in your innovation, you must have, in advance, a mental diagram of all the features that you may have to address. Our 'classroom ecology' metaphor is a useful alternative to the phrase 'systemic reform'. The overtones of the latter, of the well-oiled machine with discrete but smoothly-interconnecting parts, may be less helpful than the ecology image, with its suggestions of complex and multiple connections in a system in which you may not understand the connections until the consequences of changing them come back to haunt you. (Black and Atkin, 1996, p. 191)

This may be seen to sum up the messages about the complexity and interrelatedness of the issues which have been stressed earlier in this chapter.

The main message is that changes have to be planned with great care if errors and grief are to be avoided. A most serious source of policy errors can arise through a conjunction between the limited perspectives of policy makers and the limited power of those closest to the reality of the practices and contexts in which change is to be effected:

> If we accept a systemic view (and most people do), our actions will depend on our place in the system. This is where many of today's educational arguments and conflicts begin. Most current systemic views are through the telephoto lens. How do the schools look from the national capital? From the ministry? From the office of a provincial or regional governor? The vantage point makes a difference. The long-distance view tends to fortify the power and prerogatives of those with the most general responsibilities, and weaken the prerogatives of those closest to the sites where educational services are actually provided. (*Ibid.*, p. 197)

Here again, most readers, particularly classroom teachers in the UK, will be able to illustrate the force of this passage with examples taken from their experiences of change in assessment, and in this respect assessment and testing are no different from any other focus of educational change.

An academic study of assessment should provide an understanding of the many perspectives which are intertwined within the formulation and operation of policy and practice in this arena of education. Further, it should help one to formulate one's own appraisal of the needs for change and of the priorities within such an agenda. It is hoped that this book will help the reader to achieve both of these aims.

What is then needed is to decide whether and how to forge one's own path of contribution. This calls for thought about issues which lie outside the boundaries of this book — the brief allusion to the broader issues of innovation and change in this last section will serve only to draw attention to this wider agenda.

References

BLACK, P. and ATKIN, J.M. (eds) (1996) *Changing the Subject: Innovations in Science, Mathematics and Technology Education*, London: Routledge.

DARLING-HAMMOND, L., ANCESS, J. and FALK, B. (eds) (1995) *Authentic Assessment in Action Studies of Schools and Students at Work*, New York: Teachers College Press.

SHEPARD, L.A. (1992) 'Commentary: What policy makers who mandate tests should know about the new psychology of intellectual ability and learning', in GIFFORD, B.R. and O'CONNOR, M.C. (eds) *Changing Assessments: Alternative Views of Aptitude, Achievement and Instruction*, Boston and Dordrecht: Kluwer, pp. 301–28.

Appendix: A Little Statistics

A Little Help

What is given below is a minimal glossary to help those readers who have difficulty with the meaning of basic terms in statistics which are used in this book. It may be superfluous for anyone who has studied statistics at some time and remembered a little of what they tried to learn. There are numerous textbooks of statistics in which these matters may be followed up in detail. For those who want a starter text which does not make heavy demands on mathematical background, a suitable text would be: ERICKSON, B.H. and NOSANCHUK, T.A. (1992) *Understanding Data* (Second edition), Buckingham, Open University Press.

Mean and Spread

Table A.1 shows a possible set of examination scores from a group of 100 pupils. The teacher's list of 100 individual scores has been summarized by dividing the score range (0 to 100) into a set of bands, each 10 marks wide (except for those at each end), and counting the number of pupils with scores within each band.

For example, between scores of 15 and 24, there might have been 4 pupils with scores of 16, 19, 24 and 24 respectively — these have been represented approximately by saying that there are 4 pupils in the range 15 to 24. Thus, *Table A.1* is a summary of the total set of 100 scores, and this summary can then be represented visually by plotting the numbers in a bar chart, as shown in *Figure A.1*.

Figure A.1 shows the distribution of the scores. It can be seen that the mean score is around 50. However, *Figure A.1* also shows how widely the scores are spread. It can be seen that about two-thirds of the pupils scored between 40 and 60. In a different examination, these same pupils might have obtained results as in *Figure A.2*, having a lower mean but about the same spread, or as in *Figure A.3* having about the same mean and a narrower spread. Thus the mean and the spread are the two characteristics that serve to describe what a distribution is like.

Table A.1: Scores of 100 pupils in one examination — grouped together to give numbers in each interval of 10 marks

Score interval	0 to 4	5 to 14	15 to 24	25 to 34	35 to 44	45 to 54	55 to 64	65 to 74	75 to 84	85 to 94	95 to 99
Numbers of pupils	0	2	4	11	19	27	22	9	5	1	0

Figure A.1: Score distribution for data in Table A.1

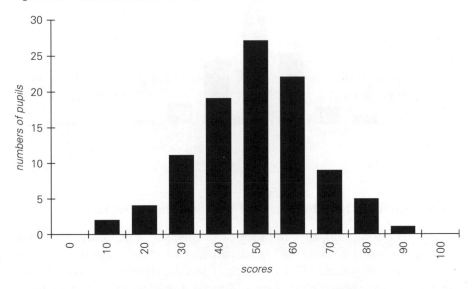

Figure A.2: Score distribution with a lower mean

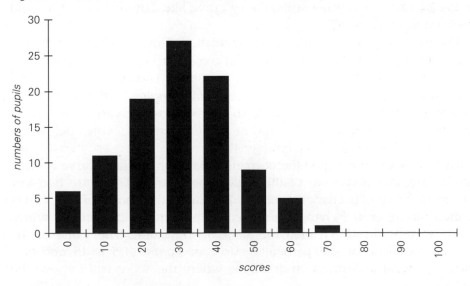

Figure A.3: Score distribution with a smaller spread

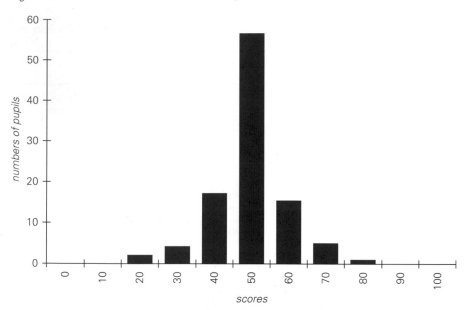

The Normal Distribution and the Standard Deviation

If there had been a much larger number of pupils, say 400, taking the same examination, but getting the same mean and spread, then there would have been a large number getting any one mark. Then the distribution could have been plotted on a finer scale of marks. *Figure A.4* shows the sort of thing that might have been obtained. It begins to look more like a smooth curve than a bar chart. If the numbers were even larger, and the scale of marks sub-divided on an even finer scale, then a curve like that in *Figure A.5* could have been obtained[1].

Many distributions in which data are scattered around a mean follow a curve of this shape. Statistical theory can explain this and can be used to work out a general algebraic formula for the curve. The curve in *Figure A.5* was drawn using this formula. The theory only applies if the data satisfy certain conditions. One of the conditions is that positive variations (scores above the mean in our example) and negative variations (scores below the mean) should be equally frequent.

This distribution is called the normal distribution, and the curve is often referred to as the bell-curve or the bell-shaped curve. There are two key terms in the formula, changing one will change the mean of the curve, changing the other will change the spread. The term in the formula which determines the spread is called the standard deviation. The value of the standard deviation for the particular curve in *Figure A.5* is 15 and two vertical lines have been drawn at values where the score is 15 above the

Figure A.4: *Score distribution with larger numbers in each score band*

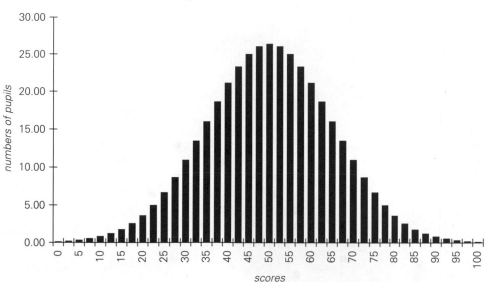

Figure A.5: *The normal distribution*

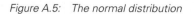

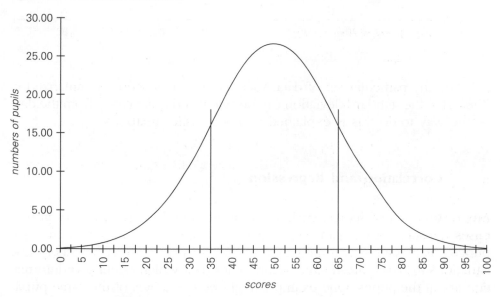

mean (i.e. at a score of 65) and 15 below the mean (i.e. at a score of 35). If the distribution is a normal one, about two thirds of the pupils' scores will lie within these two limits, leaving about one-sixth above the upper limit and one sixth below the lower limit. For a normal distribution, the proportions within any other limits can be calculated from the formula. For example, about 95 per cent of the scores will lie within two standard deviations, i.e. in this case between 30 below the mean and 30 above it.

Figure A.6:   *Correlation between two sets of scores r = 0.90*

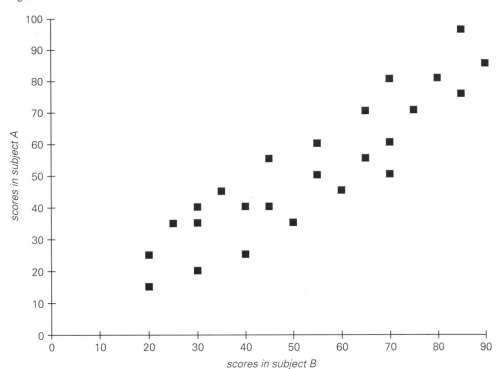

For any particular set of data, such as the set of scores summarized in
Table A.1, the standard deviation can be calculated quite easily from the data
— the way to do this is explained in any statistics textbook.

Correlation and Regression

Any distribution of scores, such as those illustrated in the diagrams above,
raises questions. How can we explain or predict the different scores that
pupils obtain? One way to help answer this question is to see whether these
variations in scores are related to any other data which might give information about the pupils. One example might be the scores of the same pupils
on an earlier examination, or the scores obtained in another, possibly related, subject, or the results of an IQ test. If any one of these ideas were to
be followed up, the data obtained would then be two sets of scores, one pair
for each pupil: for example, a pupil's score on an examination taken a year
ago and his score on a recent examination. These could be examined visually by plotting a graph with one of the scores on the horizontal axis and
another on the vertical axis. Two possible graphs of this type are shown in
Figures A.6 and A.7. Each point on one of these graphs represents the two

Figure A.7: Correlation between two sets of scores r = 0.50

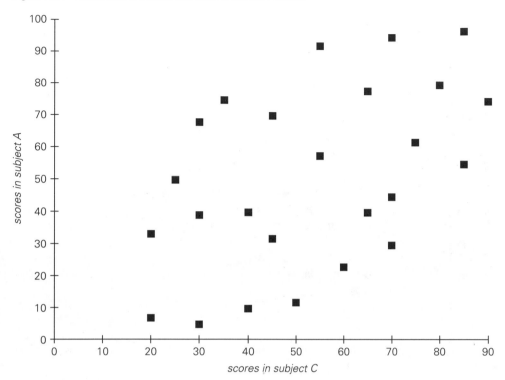

scores of a pupil. Thus the highest point in *Figure A.6* shows that one pupil scored 95 in subject A and 85 in subject B, whilst the highest point in *Figure A.7* shows a pupil who scored 97 in subject A and 85 in subject C. There are 25 points on each graph, representing the pairs of scores for 25 pupils.

It is clear that there is a stronger relationship in *Figure A.6*, i.e. between the scores in subject A and those in subject B, than in *Figure A.7*, between A and C. A numerical measure of this relationship is given by the correlation coefficient. The coefficient for the two sets of scores shown here are 0.9 for *Figure A.6* and 0.5 for *Figure A.7*. If the points were perfectly related, they would all lie on a perfect straight line; then the correlation coefficient would be 1.0. If they were scattered entirely at random, then there would be no relationship and the coefficient would be zero.

For the examples shown here, the correlations are positive, i.e. each score tends to go up as the other goes up. There can be relationships in which one score or measure goes down as the other goes up — this might be expected, for example, for a graph of the number of times a pupil failed to hand in homework against score in an examination. Then the correlation can be negative.

The correlation coefficient for a set of pairs of scores can easily be calculated from formulae available in the text-books. There are however

Figure A.8:   *Regression line of scores in subject A on those in subject B*

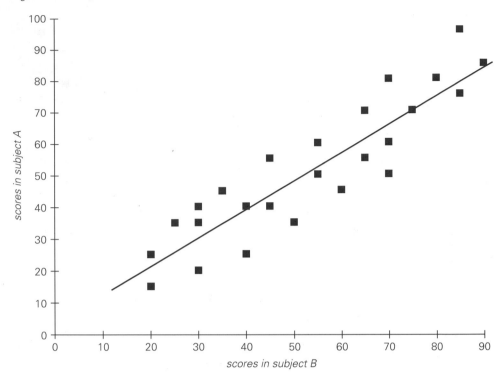

different versions of a correlation coefficient, suitable for different types of data (e.g. if we recorded for pupils a number according to their rank order in a test rather than according to the marks they scored).

Imagine that subject A was an A-level and B and C were two GCSE scores. If a teacher wished to predict the A-level score from the GCSE results, then she might draw graphs such as those in *Figures A.6 and A.7* for pupils in previous years for whom she had both the GCSE scores and the A-level results, and then try to use these graphs to predict A-level results for pupils who had just obtained their GCSEs. It is clear that the scores in subject B would be a better predictor than those in C. However, neither would be a perfect predictor. *Figure A.8* illustrates how the best possible prediction might be made. The straight line is drawn to represent the overall tendency of the relationship between the scores, and ignores the scatter of the points which makes the relationship less than perfect. Using this line, one could look up any score in B and then read off the graph the predicted score in A. There are specific rules about how to draw the best possible line, and a line drawn in this way is called a regression line. Strictly, it is the regression of A on B — i.e. the line one should use to predict A given one knew B. If the aim was the other way round, i.e. to predict B from A, the line would come out differently.

Statistical investigation of this sort is not restricted to looking at relationships between pairs of numbers. It is possible to look at pairs where one is a number and the other a category — e.g. male or female, or between two sets of categories e.g. race and socio-economic status. Indeed, in real practice the graphs of *Figures A.6 and A.7* would have to be drawn using categories — the GCSE and A-level grades — rather than numerical scores. It is also possible to look at interrelationships between three, four or more sets of data and obtain more complex indicators of relationships.

Whilst correlation data can give useful and thought-provoking clues about how outcomes might be determined, they cannot prove causal relationships. In some cases this is obvious e.g. the correlation between children's height and their size of shoe does not prove that increased height causes bigger feet or vice versa — in this case the two variables are related because they are both affected by other common factors. There are many cases where people make the logical leap from the fact of a correlation to the inference of a cause without even noticing that they have done so, and the fallacy involved can only be spotted by those with statistical vigilance.

Note

1   The vertical scale on *Figure A.5* is arbitrary — this scale is not of the same type as that in *Figure A.4*. The reason for this need not be looked into for our present purpose. The difference between the two arises because the diagram has been changed from a picture of a set of discrete bars in *Figure A.4* to a graph of a continuous curve in *Figure A.5*.

Index

testing, 17–20
training, 118
universities, 8, 10–11, 29, 30
University of London, 11

validity, 37–55, 42–53, 91–2, 155–6
variation, 39, 39–41
vocational systems, 16–17

Wales, 13, 29, 45–8, 140, 146
Werthman, C., 133
Wiliam, D., 75
Wood, R., 37–8, 53, 68, 86,
    115
working class, 12

Zola, J., 132